Title:

Navigating the AI Frontier: A Toolkit for Machine Learning Researchers

Table of Contents:

Chapter 1: Foundations of Intelligence

The Building Blocks of ML

Alex: You know, when diving into machine learning, it's essential to start with the right foundations. What do you think is the most crucial part?

Jamie: Absolutely! The core libraries and frameworks are pivotal. For instance, TensorFlow and PyTorch have become go-tos for building deep learning models. TensorFlow is fantastic for scalability, while PyTorch offers that dynamic computational graph, which is a game-changer for researchers.

Alex: And then there's Scikit-learn, which is perfect for traditional algorithms. It makes classification, regression, and clustering feel almost effortless.

Jamie: Right! Plus, Keras simplifies the process even further. It's built on TensorFlow and really streamlines model building. It's user-friendly, especially for those who are just starting out.

Beyond the Basics

Alex: Once we've got the core libraries down, what's next on the journey?

Jamie: Data manipulation and analysis are vital. Tools like Pandas and NumPy allow for efficient data handling and numerical operations. And for larger datasets, Dask comes into play—perfect for parallel computing!

Alex: Sounds like a solid plan! Having a good grip on data is critical before jumping into model training.

Chapter 2: The Art of Visualization

Painting the Picture

Jamie: Speaking of data, let's talk visualization! You can't underestimate the power of clear graphics when presenting your findings.

Alex: Exactly! Matplotlib is a classic for creating various types of plots. But if you want something more visually appealing, Seaborn offers a high-level interface that makes statistical graphics stunning.

Jamie: And for interactive visualizations, Plotly is the way to go. It's fantastic for exploratory data analysis and makes it easy to share insights.

Making Data Talk

Alex: It's fascinating how visualization can help convey complex ideas simply. So, what about the next step—applying these visualizations in specific fields?

Jamie: That's where things get exciting! In NLP, for instance, tools like NLTK and SpaCy are incredibly useful. They provide resources for processing language data, while Transformers from Hugging Face offer state-of-the-art models.

Alex: It's amazing how accessible advanced NLP techniques have become!

Chapter 3: Building and Deploying Solutions

The Computer Vision Revolution

Jamie: Moving on to computer vision—OpenCV is essential here. It has a comprehensive range of algorithms for tasks from image processing to object detection.

Alex: And FastAI builds on PyTorch, making it super simple to train neural networks for image classification. It's all about reducing the barrier to entry.

The Deployment Challenge

Jamie: Once models are built, deploying them can be tricky. That's where tools like Docker come in, right?

Alex: Exactly! Docker helps containerize applications, ensuring they run consistently across different environments. And for serving models, Flask or FastAPI are lightweight options for building APIs.

Jamie: And don't forget TensorFlow Serving, specifically designed for deploying TensorFlow models!

Chapter 4: The Ethical Frontier

Experimentation and Improvement

Alex: Now, let's discuss the importance of experiment tracking. Tools like MLflow and Weights & Biases help manage the ML lifecycle effectively, right?

Jamie: Yes! They allow you to track experiments and version datasets, making it easier to collaborate and reproduce results.

Embracing Responsibility

Alex: And in today's world, ethics in AI is paramount. Libraries like AIF360 and Fairlearn help assess and mitigate bias in ML models.

Jamie: Absolutely! They ensure that we are not just building models but are also accountable for their fairness and impact on society.

Final Thoughts

Alex: This toolkit covers so many aspects of ML and AI research. Depending on your focus—be it NLP, computer vision, or reinforcement learning—you can prioritize the tools that suit you best.

Jamie: And staying updated with the latest developments is crucial. The landscape is always evolving, and we must adapt to harness the full potential of these technologies.

Alex: It's an exciting time to be in this field! Here's to navigating the AI frontier together!

Chapter 1: Foundations of Intelligence

The Building Blocks of ML

Setting the Stage for Machine Learning

Alex: You know, when diving into machine learning, it's essential to start with the right foundations. What do you think is the most crucial part?

Jamie: Absolutely! The core libraries and frameworks are pivotal. When we think about machine learning, we immediately think of the tools that will allow us to build, train, and deploy our models effectively.

Core Libraries and Frameworks

TensorFlow: The Powerhouse of Scalability

Alex: Let's kick off with TensorFlow. It's an open-source framework developed by Google that's become synonymous with deep learning.

Jamie: Right! TensorFlow provides a robust ecosystem that supports not just neural networks but also various other machine learning algorithms. Its scalability is one of its biggest strengths, making it suitable for large-scale production applications.

Alex: What about its architecture? I've heard that its computational graph is a key feature.

Jamie: Exactly! TensorFlow employs a static computational graph, which means you define the graph first and then run it. This can lead to optimizations that make the model faster, especially for production environments. However, it can also add complexity during development.

PyTorch: Flexibility for Research

Alex: Speaking of complexity, that's where PyTorch comes in, right? It's favored for its flexibility.

Jamie: Yes! PyTorch uses a dynamic computational graph, which allows you to change the graph on the fly. This feature is particularly beneficial for research, where experimentation is key.

Alex: So, researchers can easily tweak their models and instantly see the effects?

Jamie: Precisely! It makes debugging more intuitive as well. You can use Python's debugging tools directly, which is a significant advantage over static graph systems.

Scikit-learn: The Traditional ML Toolkit

Alex: Now, what about Scikit-learn? It seems to be the go-to library for traditional algorithms.

Jamie: Scikit-learn is indeed fantastic for classic machine learning tasks. It provides a consistent interface for various algorithms, making it easy to switch between models for classification, regression, and clustering.

Alex: I love how it abstracts many complexities away. It feels almost effortless to implement algorithms like decision trees or support vector machines.

Jamie: Absolutely! And it's well-documented, which makes it a great resource for newcomers and experienced practitioners alike.

Keras: Simplifying Neural Network Building

Alex: I've also heard a lot about Keras. It's mentioned often alongside TensorFlow.

Jamie: Keras is a high-level neural networks API that runs on top of TensorFlow. It provides a user-friendly interface that allows you to build and train models with -mal code.

Alex: That's a huge plus for beginners. It can be overwhelming to dive straight into TensorFlow's complexities.

Jamie: Exactly! Keras abstracts away many of the technical details, enabling users to focus on model design and experimentation. It's a perfect entry point into deep learning.

Beyond the Basics

The Importance of Data Manipulation

Alex: Once we've got the core libraries down, what's next on the journey?

Jamie: Data manipulation and analysis are vital. Before diving into model training, it's essential to understand and prepare your data. Tools like Pandas and NumPy are invaluable for this.

Pandas: The Data Manipulation Expert

Alex: Let's start with Pandas. What makes it such a crucial tool?

Jamie: Pandas offers powerful data structures like DataFrames, which make it easy to handle structured data. You can perform operations like filtering, grouping, and merging effortlessly.

Alex: It sounds like a game-changer for data wrangling.

Jamie: It truly is! You can import data from various sources, clean it, and prepare it for analysis—all in a user-friendly way.

NumPy: The Numerical Foundation

Alex: And then there's NumPy, right? What role does it play?

Jamie: NumPy is the foundation for numerical operations in Python. It provides support for multi-dimensional arrays and matrices, along with a collection of mathematical functions to operate on these data structures.

Alex: So, it's particularly useful for mathematical computations and linear algebra, which are central to many ML algorithms.

Jamie: Exactly! NumPy is often used under the hood by other libraries, including Pandas, TensorFlow, and PyTorch.

Dask: Handling Larger Datasets

Alex: For larger datasets, I believe Dask comes into play. How does it fit into the picture?

Jamie: Dask is designed for parallel computing, allowing you to handle datasets that don't fit into memory. It breaks data into smaller chunks and processes them in parallel, making it a great choice for big data applications.

Alex: That sounds incredibly useful. Scaling up is always a challenge, especially with the volume of data we encounter today.

Emphasizing Data Understanding

Jamie: Having a good grip on data is critical before jumping into model training. It's important to understand the nuances of your dataset, including its structure, missing values, and distributions.

Alex: So, exploratory data analysis (EDA) is essential, right?

Jamie: Exactly! EDA allows you to visualize your data and uncover underlying patterns. Using visualization libraries like Matplotlib and Seaborn can greatly enhance this process.

Visualizing Data for Insights

Alex: Let's touch on visualization briefly. Why is it so important?

Jamie: Visualization helps in understanding data relationships and distributions, guiding feature selection and engineering decisions. It can also reveal anomalies or outliers that might affect model performance.

Alex: So, using visualization tools can enhance our modelling efforts significantly?

Jamie: Absolutely! For instance, Seaborn provides attractive statistical graphics that help in visualizing distributions and relationships between variables, while Matplotlib offers more customization options for complex visualizations.

The Journey Ahead

Alex: It's clear that laying the right foundation is crucial. From understanding core libraries to mastering data manipulation, every step prepares us for building effective models.

Jamie: Exactly! As we move forward, we'll delve deeper into specific domains like natural language processing, computer vision, and reinforcement learning, each with its unique set of tools and techniques.

Alex: I'm excited to explore those areas. It feels like we're just scratching the surface of what's possible in machine learning!

Jamie: Definitely! The landscape of ML and AI is vast and continually evolving. Mastering these foundational skills will empower us to navigate that landscape effectively.

Conclusion

As we wrap up this chapter, remember that the journey into machine learning is as much about understanding the tools at your disposal as it is about the algorithms themselves. By building a solid foundation with the right libraries and mastering data manipulation, you're well on your way to becoming proficient in this exciting field. As we progress, we'll explore more specialized tools and techniques that will further enhance your ability to create impactful machine learning solutions.

Chapter 2:

The Art of Visualization

Painting the Picture

The Importance of Visualization

Jamie: Speaking of data, let's talk visualization! You can't underestimate the power of clear graphics when presenting your findings.

Alex: Exactly! Visualization can be a game changer. It transforms raw data into insights that are easier to understand. People often say, "A picture is worth a thousand words," and that couldn't be more true in data science.

The Classic: Matplotlib

Jamie: One of the go-to libraries for creating visualizations in Python is Matplotlib. It's incredibly versatile and allows you to create a wide range of plots.

Alex: Right! You can make line plots, scatter plots, bar charts, and even complex visualizations like 3D plots. Matplotlib provides a lot of control over the aesthetics of your plots, too.

Jamie: Absolutely! You can customize everything from colors and markers to labels and legends. However, the learning curve can be a bit steep for beginners.

The Beauty of Seaborn

Alex: That's where Seaborn comes in, right? It's built on top of Matplotlib and makes statistical graphics more attractive and easier to generate.

Jamie: Exactly! Seaborn simplifies the process of creating complex visualizations with just a few lines of code. It's especially good for visualizing relationships between variables.

Alex: The default color palettes and themes are also much more appealing. They really enhance the visual quality of the plots.

Interactive Insights with Plotly

Jamie: And for those who want interactivity, Plotly is the way to go. It allows you to create interactive plots that users can explore themselves.

Alex: That's fantastic for exploratory data analysis! Users can hover over data points to get more information or zoom in on specific areas of interest.

Jamie: Plus, Plotly integrates well with web applications, making it easy to share insights through dashboards.

Making Data Talk

Communicating Complex Ideas

Alex: It's fascinating how visualization can help convey complex ideas simply. Good visuals can make a data-driven story much more compelling.

Jamie: Definitely! For example, when presenting a regression analysis, a scatter plot with a fitted line can quickly show trends, outliers, and the overall relationship between variables.

Visualization in Specific Fields

Alex: So, what about applying these visualizations in specific fields? How do we tailor our visualizations based on the context?

Jamie: That's where things get exciting! In natural language processing (NLP), for instance, we can use visualizations to analyze text data.

Alex: Right! Tools like NLTK and SpaCy are incredibly useful for processing language data, but how do we visualize the results?

Visualizing NLP Results

Jamie: One common technique is to use word clouds to show the frequency of words in a corpus. It gives a quick visual representation of what terms are most prominent.

Alex: That's a fun way to visualize text data! What about sentiment analysis? Can visualization help there, too?

Jamie: Absolutely! You can create bar charts or pie charts to represent the distribution of sentiments—positive, negative, and neutral—across a dataset. It's a straightforward way to communicate the overall sentiment of a large amount of text.

Advanced NLP Visualization

Alex: What about more advanced techniques? Can we visualize relationships in language data?

Jamie: Yes! You can use techniques like t-SNE or PCA to reduce dimensionality of word embeddings, allowing you to visualize clusters of similar words or phrases in a two-dimensional space.

Alex: That sounds powerful! It must reveal interesting insights into language structure and meaning.

Jamie: It really does! Clustering similar words can highlight semantic relationships, which is incredibly valuable for understanding language nuances.

A New Frontier: Transformers and Visualization

Alex: And speaking of advanced techniques, I've heard a lot about Transformers and their impact on NLP.

Jamie: Absolutely! The Transformers library from Hugging Face provides access to state-of-the-art pre-trained models, making it easier to implement complex NLP tasks.

Alex: How do we visualize the results from these models?

Jamie: For instance, you can visualize attention weights to understand which words the model focuses on while making predictions. Heatmaps can effectively display these weights, revealing how the model interprets context.

Alex: That's a great way to demystify the model's decision-making process!

Bringing It All Together

The Power of Storytelling

Jamie: Ultimately, effective visualization isn't just about creating pretty pictures; it's about telling a story with your data. You want your audience to grasp the key insights at a glance.

Alex: Agreed! Each visualization should have a clear purpose and contribute to the overall narrative.

Best Practices for Effective Visualization

Jamie: Here are a few best practices to keep in mind when visualizing data:

1. **Know Your Audience:** Tailor your visualizations to the audience's level of expertise.
2. **Choose the Right Type of Plot:** Different types of data require different visualization techniques.
3. **Simplify:** Avoid clutter. A clean, straightforward design enhances comprehension.
4. **Use Color Wisely:** Colors should enhance, not distract. Consistent color schemes help convey information effectively.
5. **Label Clearly:** Ensure axes, legends, and titles are clearly labeled to provide context.

Alex: Those are solid guidelines! It's essential to keep the audience in mind throughout the visualization process.

Conclusion

Jamie: As we wrap up this chapter on visualization, remember that effective data representation can significantly enhance your machine learning projects. By mastering tools like Matplotlib, Seaborn, and Plotly, and understanding how to apply these visualizations in fields like NLP, you'll be better equipped to communicate insights and drive decision-making.

Alex: I can't wait to explore the practical applications of these concepts in our upcoming projects. Visualization truly is an art, and mastering it will set us apart as data practitioners!

Chapter 3: Building and Deploying Solutions

The Computer Vision Revolution

Introduction to Computer Vision

Jamie: Moving on to computer vision—this field has truly revolutionized how we interact with technology. With advancements in deep learning, machines can now interpret and understand visual data.

Alex: It's fascinating how far we've come! OpenCV is essential here. It has a comprehensive range of algorithms for tasks from image processing to object detection.

Exploring OpenCV

Jamie: OpenCV, or Open Source Computer Vision Library, is a highly efficient library that supports numerous computer vision tasks. It provides functions for image manipulation, feature extraction, and even real-time video processing.

Alex: What kind of tasks can we accomplish with OpenCV?

Jamie: You can do a lot! For instance, you can perform face detection, object tracking, image filtering, and edge detection, among others. Its versatility makes it a staple for anyone working in computer vision.

FastAI: Simplifying Neural Networks

Alex: And FastAI builds on PyTorch, making it super simple to train neural networks for image classification. It's all about reducing the barrier to entry.

Jamie: Exactly! FastAI abstracts away much of the complexity of deep learning, allowing users to focus on the higher-level concepts rather than getting bogged down in the implementation details.

Alex: This is particularly useful for those new to the field. FastAI provides high-level components that can be easily customized.

Training Models with FastAI

Jamie: FastAI's Learner class simplifies the training process. You can load your data, define a model, and start training with just a few lines of code. It also includes built-in support for techniques like transfer learning, which is crucial for effective model training.

Alex: That's a huge time-saver! Plus, FastAI offers powerful data augmentation techniques, which can enhance model performance by artificially expanding the training dataset.

The Deployment Challenge

The Importance of Deployment

Jamie: Once models are built, deploying them can be tricky. Many researchers struggle with transitioning their models from the development phase to production.

Alex: That's a crucial step! A model is only as good as its deployment. It needs to work in real-world scenarios, which often means addressing issues of scalability, reliability, and performance.

Containerization with Docker

Jamie: That's where tools like Docker come in, right?

Alex: Exactly! Docker helps containerize applications, ensuring they run consistently across different environments. You can package your model, its dependencies, and the runtime environment into a single container.

Jamie: This approach eliminates the classic "it works on my machine" problem. Once your application is containerized, you can run it anywhere Docker is supported.

Building APIs with Flask and FastAPI

Alex: For serving models, Flask and FastAPI are lightweight options for building APIs. They allow you to create endpoints that can accept data and return predictions.

Jamie: Flask is great for smaller applications and quick prototypes, while FastAPI offers better performance and automatic generation of API documentation thanks to its use of Python type hints.

Alex: FastAPI's asynchronous capabilities are a huge advantage, especially when dealing with high loads or multiple requests simultaneously.

TensorFlow Serving

Jamie: And don't forget TensorFlow Serving, specifically designed for deploying TensorFlow models! It provides a robust framework for serving machine learning models in production environments.

Alex: TensorFlow Serving allows for easy integration with TensorFlow models, providing features like versioning, logging, and monitoring, which are critical for maintaining model performance in production.

The Deployment Workflow

Jamie: So, what does the workflow look like for deploying a machine learning model?

Alex: Generally, it involves several steps:

1. **Model Training:** First, you build and train your model using a suitable framework.
2. **Model Serialization:** Save the model in a format that can be loaded later (like TensorFlow's SavedModel format or PyTorch's TorchScript).
3. **Containerization:** Package the model and its dependencies into a Docker container.
4. **API Development:** Create an API using Flask or FastAPI to serve the model.
5. **Deployment:** Finally, deploy the containerized application on a cloud service or server.

Jamie: That's a clear pathway! It's essential to automate this process as much as possible, using CI/CD pipelines to streamline updates and deployments.

Monitoring and Maintenance

Alex: After deployment, monitoring the model's performance is crucial. We need to ensure it continues to function as expected in production.

Jamie: Absolutely! Monitoring can help you catch issues early, such as model drift, where the model's performance degrades due to changes in data patterns. Tools like Prometheus and Grafana can help with this.

Alex: Regular maintenance, including retraining the model with new data, is also important to keep it relevant and effective.

Conclusion

Jamie: As we conclude this chapter, remember that building and deploying machine learning models requires careful planning and execution. From leveraging libraries like OpenCV and FastAI for development to using Docker and API frameworks for deployment, each step is crucial for success.

Alex: It's a fascinating journey, and mastering these skills will empower us to turn our ideas into reality. The ability to deploy models effectively is what truly bridges the gap between research and real-world application. I'm excited to see where this knowledge takes us!

Chapter 4: The Ethical Frontier

Experimentation and Improvement

The Importance of Experiment Tracking

Alex: Now, let's discuss the importance of experiment tracking. In machine learning, being able to document and manage experiments is crucial for reproducibility and collaboration.

Jamie: Absolutely! Tools like MLflow and Weights & Biases have become essential in managing the ML lifecycle effectively. They allow you to track experiments, visualize metrics, and version datasets.

Getting Started with MLflow

Alex: MLflow is a comprehensive platform. It offers a centralized hub where you can log parameters, metrics, and artifacts from your experiments.

Jamie: Exactly! With MLflow, you can also register models and manage different versions. This feature is invaluable when you need to compare models or revert to a previous version.

Alex: Plus, MLflow provides a UI that makes it easy to visualize your experiments. You can quickly identify which parameters yielded the best results.

Weights & Biases for Collaboration

Jamie: On the other hand, Weights & Biases is fantastic for team collaboration. It helps you keep track of experiments, but its dashboard is particularly useful for sharing insights with team members.

Alex: Right! You can create visualizations that showcase model performance over time, making it easier to communicate findings. And since it integrates with most popular ML frameworks, it fits seamlessly into existing workflows.

The Feedback Loop

Jamie: The real strength of these tools lies in their ability to create a feedback loop. By tracking experiments, you can continually refine your models and improve performance based on empirical evidence.

Alex: This iterative process is vital for success in machine learning. The more you experiment and track results, the better your understanding of the model's behavior becomes.

Embracing Responsibility

The Ethical Landscape of AI

Jamie: Now, shifting gears a bit, let's talk about ethics in AI. In today's world, this is paramount. As machine learning practitioners, we have a responsibility to ensure our models are fair and ethical.

Alex: Absolutely! Bias can creep into models in many ways, whether it's through biased training data or flawed algorithms. This can lead to unfair outcomes that disproportionately affect certain groups.

Tools for Fairness: AIF360

Jamie: Libraries like AIF360 (AI Fairness 360) provide tools to assess and mitigate bias in machine learning models. It includes metrics to evaluate model fairness and algorithms to reduce bias in both training and inference.

Alex: That's crucial! AIF360 offers a comprehensive suite of fairness metrics that help identify potential issues before deploying a model. This proactive approach can help prevent harm.

Fairlearn for Mitigating Bias

Jamie: Another valuable toolkit is Fairlearn, which focuses on assessing and mitigating unfairness in machine learning. It allows you to visualize fairness metrics and compare different model outcomes based on protected attributes.

Alex: Fairlearn provides strategies for mitigating bias, such as adjusting the decision thresholds or re-weighting the training data. This flexibility is essential for addressing fairness issues in real-world applications.

Accountability and Transparency

Jamie: But tools alone aren't enough. We need to foster a culture of accountability and transparency in AI development.

Alex: Definitely! This means documenting decision-making processes, being transparent about model limitations, and actively engaging with stakeholders.

Ethical Considerations in Deployment

Jamie: When deploying models, it's important to consider the potential societal impact. How will the model be used, and what are the implications for different groups?

Alex: Engaging with communities affected by these models can provide invaluable insights and help identify potential biases early on.

Continuous Learning and Adaptation

Jamie: Ethical AI isn't a one-time effort. It requires continuous learning and adaptation. As our understanding of fairness and bias evolves, so should our models and practices.

Alex: Agreed! Ongoing education about the ethical implications of our work is vital. This helps ensure that we're not just technically proficient but also socially responsible.

Conclusion

Jamie: As we conclude this chapter on the ethical frontier, remember that our role as ML practitioners extends beyond technical skills. We must strive to build fair, accountable, and transparent systems.

Alex: Absolutely! By leveraging tools like MLflow, Weights & Biases, AIF360, and Fairlearn, we can create a more ethical landscape in AI. This commitment to responsible AI practices will help us build models that positively impact society.

Jamie: Let's continue to champion ethics in our work, ensuring that our innovations serve all members of society fairly and justly. The future of AI depends on our choices today!

Final Thoughts

Embracing the Journey Ahead

Alex: This toolkit covers so many aspects of ML and AI research. Depending on your focus—be it NLP, computer vision, or reinforcement learning—you can prioritize the tools that suit you best.

Jamie: Exactly! Each area has its unique challenges and opportunities, and understanding the right tools to use can make all the difference. It's about finding what works for you and your specific projects.

The Importance of Lifelong Learning

Alex: And staying updated with the latest developments is crucial. The landscape is always evolving, and we must adapt to harness the full potential of these technologies.

Jamie: Continuous learning is essential! New libraries, frameworks, and techniques emerge all the time. Engaging with the community, attending conferences, and participating in online courses can keep us on the cutting edge.

The Excitement of Innovation

Alex: It's an exciting time to be in this field! With advancements in AI, we're not just creating smarter algorithms—we're reshaping industries and improving lives.

Jamie: Absolutely! The potential for innovation is immense. From healthcare to education, AI has the power to transform how we approach complex problems.

Navigating the AI Frontier

Alex: Here's to navigating the AI frontier together! As we explore, let's keep our focus on ethical considerations and the broader impact of our work.

Jamie: Agreed! Our responsibility is to ensure that our innovations are fair, transparent, and beneficial to all. Let's be pioneers in creating a positive future for AI.

Moving Forward

Alex: So, whether you're just starting your journey in ML or you're a seasoned expert, remember that collaboration and community are key. We're all in this together!

Jamie: Yes! Let's embrace the challenges ahead with curiosity and dedication. The journey in AI is just beginning, and the possibilities are endless!

An AI toolkit for machine learning (ML) and AI researchers involves compiling a variety of libraries, frameworks, and tools that facilitate research, experimentation, and deployment. Here's a comprehensive toolkit categorized by functionality:

1. Core Libraries and Frameworks

- **TensorFlow**: An open-source framework for building ML models, particularly deep learning.
- **PyTorch**: A dynamic computational graph framework favoured for research due to its flexibility and ease of use.
- **Scikit-learn**: A robust library for traditional ML algorithms, including classification, regression, and clustering.
- **Keras**: A high-level neural networks API that runs on top of TensorFlow, simplifying model building.

2. Data Manipulation and Analysis

- **Pandas**: Essential for data manipulation and analysis, offering data structures like DataFrames.
- **NumPy**: Provides support for numerical operations and is foundational for many ML libraries.
- **Dask**: For parallel computing and handling large datasets that don't fit into memory.

3. Visualization Tools

- **Matplotlib**: A plotting library for creating static, interactive, and animated visualizations.
- **Seaborn**: Built on Matplotlib, it provides a high-level interface for drawing attractive statistical graphics.
- **Plotly**: For interactive plots and dashboards, useful for exploratory data analysis.

4. Natural Language Processing (NLP)

- **NLTK**: A toolkit for working with human language data, providing easy access to lexical resources.
- **SpaCy**: A library designed for efficient NLP tasks with pre-trained models.
- **Transformers (Hugging Face)**: For state-of-the-art pre-trained models in NLP, providing an easy way to fine-tune models.

5. Computer Vision

- **OpenCV**: A library for computer vision tasks that includes a wide range of algorithms.
- **FastAI**: Built on PyTorch, it simplifies training neural networks for image classification and other tasks.

6. Model Deployment and Serving

- **Docker**: For containerizing applications, ensuring consistency across environments.
- **Flask/FastAPI**: Lightweight web frameworks for building APIs to serve models.
- **TensorFlow Serving**: Specifically designed for serving TensorFlow models in production.

7. Experiment Tracking and Management

- **MLflow**: An open-source platform for managing the ML lifecycle, including experimentation, reproducibility, and deployment.
- **Weights & Biases**: A tool for experiment tracking, dataset versioning, and collaborative reporting.

8. Hyperparameter Tuning

- **Optuna**: A hyperparameter optimization framework that automates the tuning process.
- **Ray Tune**: Scalable hyperparameter tuning that works seamlessly with popular ML libraries.

9. Reinforcement Learning

- **OpenAI Gym**: A toolkit for developing and comparing reinforcement learning algorithms.

- **Stable Baselines3**: Implementations of RL algorithms based on PyTorch, making it easier to work with.

10. Research and Collaboration Tools

- **Jupyter Notebooks**: Interactive notebooks for documenting and sharing research.
- **Git**: Version control for code and collaboration on projects.
- **Google Colab**: A cloud-based Jupyter notebook service that provides free access to GPUs.

11. Ethics and Fairness Tools

- **AIF360 (AI Fairness 360)**: A library for detecting and mitigating bias in ML models.
- **Fairlearn**: A toolkit for assessing and mitigating unfairness in ML.

12. Miscellaneous Tools

- **DVC (Data Version Control)**: For versioning datasets and machine learning models.
- **Streamlit**: For creating web apps quickly for ML projects, making it easy to showcase results.

Conclusion

This toolkit is designed to cover various aspects of ML and AI research. Depending on your specific focus (NLP, computer vision, reinforcement learning, etc.), you may prioritize certain tools over others. Keeping abreast of new developments and libraries in the field is also essential, as the landscape is constantly evolving!

Let's dive on concepts:

TensorFlow: An In-Depth Overview

Introduction to TensorFlow

TensorFlow is an open-source machine learning framework developed by the Google Brain team. Launched in 2015, it has quickly become one of the most popular libraries for building and deploying machine learning (ML) models, particularly deep learning applications. TensorFlow provides a comprehensive ecosystem that includes libraries, tools, and community resources, making it suitable for both research and production environments.

Key Features

1. **Flexibility**: TensorFlow supports various programming languages (Python, C++, JavaScript) and platforms (desktop, mobile, cloud).

2. **Scalability**: It can handle large-scale datasets and can run on multiple CPUs or GPUs, enabling efficient training of complex models.

3. **Deployment**: TensorFlow Serving, TensorFlow Lite, and TensorFlow.js allow seamless deployment of models across different environments.

4. **Ecosystem**: TensorFlow offers a suite of tools, such as TensorBoard for visualization, and TensorFlow Hub for sharing models.

Architecture of TensorFlow

The architecture of TensorFlow is designed to facilitate the development of complex ML models. It consists of several key components:

1. Tensors

At the core of TensorFlow is the concept of a tensor, a multi-dimensional array that is the fundamental data structure used for storing data. Tensors can be scalars, vectors, matrices, or higher-dimensional arrays. Operations on tensors are performed using the TensorFlow API, enabling users to manipulate and compute data efficiently.

2. Graphs

TensorFlow uses a computational graph structure, where nodes represent operations (e.g., addition, multiplication) and edges represent the data (tensors) flowing between these operations. This graph-based approach allows for optimization and parallel execution, which is essential for large-scale ML tasks.

3. Sessions

In earlier versions of TensorFlow, sessions were used to execute the computational graphs. A session encapsulates the environment in which operations are executed and manages resources like memory. While the session concept is less prominent in TensorFlow 2.x, understanding it is still valuable for grasping the library's evolution.

4. Eager Execution

With the introduction of TensorFlow 2.x, eager execution became the default mode. Eager execution allows for immediate evaluation of operations, enabling a more intuitive and interactive programming style. This is particularly beneficial for debugging and prototyping.

Key Components and Modules

1. Keras API

Keras is a high-level API integrated into TensorFlow that simplifies the process of building neural networks. It provides a user-friendly interface to create and train models. Key features include:

- **Sequential API**: For building models layer by layer in a linear stack.
- **Functional API**: For creating complex models, such as multi-input and multi-output architectures.
- **Model Subclassing**: For defining custom models by subclassing the tf.keras.Model class.

2. Optimizers

TensorFlow includes various optimization algorithms for training models. Popular optimizers include:

- **Gradient Descent**: The foundational algorithm for updating model parameters.
- **Adam**: An adaptive learning rate optimization algorithm that combines momentum and RMSprop.
- **SGD (Stochastic Gradient Descent)**: A widely used optimizer for its simplicity and effectiveness.

3. Loss Functions

Loss functions quantify the difference between the predicted and actual values, guiding the optimization process. TensorFlow provides several built-in loss functions, including:

- **Mean Squared Error**: Commonly used for regression tasks.
- **Categorical Crossentropy**: Used for multi-class classification problems.

- **Binary Crossentropy**: Used for binary classification tasks.

4. Metrics

Metrics are used to evaluate the performance of a model during training and testing. TensorFlow supports a variety of metrics, such as:

- **Accuracy**: Measures the proportion of correct predictions.
- **Precision and Recall**: Used for evaluating models in imbalanced datasets.
- **F1 Score**: A harmonic mean of precision and recall.

5. Preprocessing and Data Handling

TensorFlow provides utilities for data preprocessing and augmentation. The tf.data API allows users to build efficient input pipelines, enabling seamless data loading and preprocessing. This is crucial for handling large datasets and ensuring that the model is trained on high-quality data.

6. TensorBoard

TensorBoard is a powerful visualization tool that comes with TensorFlow. It allows users to visualize various aspects of their models, including:

- **Training Metrics**: Visualize loss and accuracy over epochs.
- **Model Graphs**: Inspect the computational graph structure.
- **Histograms**: Analyze distributions of weights and biases.

Advanced Features

1. Distributed Training

TensorFlow supports distributed training across multiple devices and clusters. This is achieved through the tf.distribute API, which simplifies the process of parallelizing training workloads. Key strategies include:

- **MirroredStrategy**: For synchronous training on multiple GPUs.
- **TPUStrategy**: For leveraging Tensor Processing Units (TPUs) in Google Cloud.

2. Transfer Learning

Transfer learning allows researchers to leverage pre-trained models on similar tasks, significantly reducing training time and resource consumption. TensorFlow Hub provides a repository of pre-trained models that can be easily integrated into custom applications.

3. Model Saving and Serialization

TensorFlow makes it easy to save and restore models. The tf.keras.Model class provides methods for saving the entire model architecture and weights, as well as the optimizer state. This enables easy deployment and sharing of models.

4. TensorFlow Extended (TFX)

TFX is an end-to-end platform for deploying production ML pipelines. It includes components for data validation, preprocessing, model validation, and serving, facilitating the transition from research to production.

Community and Ecosystem

1. Documentation and Tutorials

TensorFlow has comprehensive documentation and numerous tutorials that cater to various skill levels. The TensorFlow website provides guides, API references, and example projects, making it easier for newcomers to get started.

2. Community Support

The TensorFlow community is active and robust, with forums like Stack Overflow and GitHub issues providing platforms for troubleshooting and knowledge sharing. The TensorFlow GitHub repository hosts contributions from developers worldwide, continuously enhancing the framework.

3. Conferences and Events

Google regularly organizes TensorFlow Dev Summits, workshops, and meetups to foster collaboration and knowledge exchange among researchers and developers. These events provide insights into the latest developments and practical applications of TensorFlow.

Use Cases

1. Image Classification

TensorFlow is widely used for image classification tasks. With its support for convolutional neural networks (CNNs), researchers can build models that achieve state-of-the-art accuracy on benchmark datasets like CIFAR-10 and ImageNet.

2. Natural Language Processing

TensorFlow has robust support for NLP tasks, including text classification, sentiment analysis, and machine translation. The integration of pre-trained models from Hugging Face makes it easier to apply advanced NLP techniques.

3. Reinforcement Learning

TensorFlow is employed in reinforcement learning applications, including game AI, robotics, and autonomous systems. Its flexibility allows researchers to experiment with various algorithms and environments.

4. Time Series Analysis

With TensorFlow, researchers can model time series data using recurrent neural networks (RNNs) and long short-term memory (LSTM) networks, making it suitable for tasks like stock price prediction and weather forecasting.

Conclusion

TensorFlow has revolutionized the landscape of machine learning and deep learning. Its flexibility, scalability, and extensive ecosystem make it a preferred choice for both researchers and practitioners. With ongoing development and community support, TensorFlow continues to evolve, empowering users to tackle complex ML challenges and push the boundaries of artificial intelligence.

In summary, whether you are a newcomer to machine learning or an experienced researcher, TensorFlow provides the tools and resources necessary to develop, train, and deploy state-of-the-art models efficiently. The combination of its powerful features and a supportive community makes it an invaluable asset in the field of artificial intelligence.

PyTorch: A Comprehensive Overview

Introduction to PyTorch

PyTorch is an open-source machine learning framework developed by Facebook's AI Research lab (FAIR) and launched in 2016. It has rapidly gained popularity in the machine learning and deep learning communities, especially among researchers, due to its dynamic computational graph capabilities and user-friendly interface. PyTorch allows users to define and manipulate neural networks with unprecedented flexibility, making it ideal for both experimentation and deployment.

Key Features of PyTorch

1. **Dynamic Computation Graphs**: PyTorch constructs computation graphs on-the-fly, enabling immediate execution and debugging.

2. **Easy to Use**: Its intuitive syntax and Pythonic nature make it accessible for beginners and experienced developers alike.

3. **Robust Ecosystem**: PyTorch has a growing ecosystem of libraries and tools, such as TorchVision for computer vision tasks and TorchText for natural language processing.

4. **Strong Community Support**: The active community contributes to extensive documentation, tutorials, and forums, facilitating knowledge sharing and troubleshooting.

Architecture of PyTorch

The architecture of PyTorch is designed to provide maximum flexibility while maintaining efficiency. Key components include:

1. Tensors

At the core of PyTorch is the tensor, a multi-dimensional array similar to NumPy arrays but with additional capabilities for GPU acceleration. Tensors can be manipulated using a wide array of built-in functions and can easily transition between CPU and GPU.

2. Autograd

Autograd is PyTorch's automatic differentiation library that powers the backpropagation algorithm. It tracks operations on tensors and records the computational graph, allowing for automatic computation of gradients. This feature is essential for training deep learning models.

3. Modules and Neural Networks

PyTorch provides the torch.nn module for building neural networks. Users can define their own layers and architectures using the torch.nn.Module class. This modular design allows for the creation of complex networks by stacking layers and customizing forward and backward passes.

4. Optimizers

The torch.optim module contains various optimization algorithms, including stochastic gradient descent (SGD), Adam, and RMSprop. These optimizers facilitate the training process by adjusting model parameters based on computed gradients.

Key Components and Modules

1. Tensors and Operations

PyTorch tensors are versatile and support a wide range of operations:

- **Creation**: Tensors can be created from lists, NumPy arrays, or random values using functions like torch.tensor(), torch.zeros(), and torch.rand().
- **Manipulation**: PyTorch supports element-wise operations, matrix operations, indexing, slicing, and reshaping. Functions such as torch.add(), torch.matmul(), and torch.view() enable intuitive manipulation.

2. Autograd in Depth

Autograd is one of PyTorch's standout features, enabling automatic differentiation. Here's how it works:

- **Tracking Operations**: When a tensor with the attribute requires_grad=True undergoes operations, PyTorch builds a computation graph that records the operations and their relationships.
- **Backward Pass**: The .backward() method computes gradients of tensors with respect to some loss. This is essential for optimizing model parameters.
- **Gradient Access**: After calling backward, the gradients can be accessed via the .grad attribute of the tensor.

3. Building Neural Networks

Sequential Models

For simple architectures, PyTorch provides the torch.nn.Sequential container, which allows stacking layers in a linear fashion. For example:

python

```
code
import torch
import torch.nn as nn

model = nn.Sequential(
    nn.Linear(10, 5),
    nn.ReLU(),
    nn.Linear(5, 2)
)
```

Custom Models

For more complex architectures, users can subclass torch.nn.Module. This allows for custom forward and backward methods:

python

```
code
class MyModel(nn.Module):
    def __init__(self):
        super(MyModel, self).__init__()
        self.fc1 = nn.Linear(10, 5)
        self.fc2 = nn.Linear(5, 2)

    def forward(self, x):
        x = torch.relu(self.fc1(x))
        return self.fc2(x)
```

4. Loss Functions

PyTorch provides a variety of built-in loss functions, essential for training models. Commonly used loss functions include:

- **Mean Squared Error (MSE)**: Used for regression tasks.
- **Cross-Entropy Loss**: Typically used for classification tasks.
- **Negative Log-Likelihood**: Useful in probabilistic models.

5. Data Handling and Preprocessing

Data handling is streamlined in PyTorch through the torch.utils.data module, which includes:

- **Dataset**: A base class for creating custom datasets. Users can override the __len__() and __getitem__() methods.
- **DataLoader**: Combines a dataset and a sampler, providing an iterable over the dataset with support for batching, shuffling, and parallel data loading.

Example of using DataLoader:

python

code

```python
from torch.utils.data import DataLoader, Dataset

class MyDataset(Dataset):
    def __init__(self, data, labels):
        self.data = data
        self.labels = labels

    def __len__(self):
        return len(self.data)

    def __getitem__(self, idx):
        return self.data[idx], self.labels[idx]

dataset = MyDataset(data, labels)
dataloader = DataLoader(dataset, batch_size=32, shuffle=True)
```

6. Optimizers

The torch.optim module offers various optimizers, making it easy to choose the right one for your model:

python

code

```python
optimizer = torch.optim.Adam(model.parameters(), lr=0.001)
```

Using an optimizer typically involves:

1. Clearing gradients with optimizer.zero_grad().
2. Performing a forward pass to compute outputs.

3. Calculating the loss.
4. Performing a backward pass with loss.backward().
5. Updating parameters with optimizer.step().

Advanced Features

1. Dynamic Computation Graphs

One of the most compelling features of PyTorch is its dynamic computation graph. Unlike static graph frameworks, where the graph is defined before execution, PyTorch builds the graph dynamically as operations are executed. This allows for:

- **Debugging**: Easier to debug since you can inspect the values and the structure of the graph at any point.
- **Flexible Models**: Models can change during execution, allowing for advanced techniques like varying input sizes and dynamic architectures.

2. Transfer Learning

Transfer learning is a powerful approach where pre-trained models are adapted to new tasks. PyTorch facilitates transfer learning with built-in models in the torchvision.models module. For instance:

python

 code

```
import torchvision.models as models


model = models.resnet18(pretrained=True)
for param in model.parameters():
    param.requires_grad = False  # Freeze pre-trained layers
model.fc = nn.Linear(model.fc.in_features, num_classes)  # Modify the final layer
```

3. TorchScript

TorchScript allows you to create serializable and optimizable models from PyTorch code. It provides a way to export models for deployment, enabling them to run in a C++ runtime environment. This is beneficial for deploying models in production.

The conversion to TorchScript can be done using:

- **Tracing**: For models that do not have dynamic control flows.
- **Scripting**: For models with conditional statements and loops.

4. Distributed Training

PyTorch supports distributed training out of the box, enabling the training of models on multiple GPUs or across several machines. The torch.distributed package allows you to set up communication between processes and synchronize gradients.

Strategies include:

- **Data Parallelism**: Distributing input data across multiple GPUs.
- **Model Parallelism**: Splitting the model across GPUs.

5. Visualization with TensorBoard

PyTorch integrates with TensorBoard, a popular visualization toolkit. You can log metrics, visualize the model graph, and track training progress. PyTorch's torch.utils.tensorboard module makes this straightforward:

python

 code

```python
from torch.utils.tensorboard import SummaryWriter

writer = SummaryWriter()
writer.add_scalar('Loss/train', loss, epoch)
writer.close()
```

Community and Ecosystem

1. Documentation and Tutorials

PyTorch boasts comprehensive documentation, including a wealth of tutorials covering everything from the basics to advanced topics. The official website provides clear examples and explanations, making it accessible for users at all levels.

2. Active Community

The PyTorch community is vibrant and supportive, with numerous forums, discussion groups, and social media channels. Resources like Stack Overflow and the PyTorch forums are invaluable for troubleshooting and sharing knowledge.

3. Research and Publications

Many cutting-edge research papers and projects utilize PyTorch, reinforcing its reputation as a go-to framework for academics and industry professionals. Conferences like NeurIPS, ICML, and CVPR often feature work implemented in PyTorch.

4. Extensions and Libraries

PyTorch has a rich ecosystem of libraries that extend its functionality. Some notable libraries include:

- **TorchVision**: For computer vision tasks, providing datasets, model architectures, and image transformations.

- **TorchText**: For natural language processing, offering tools for text processing and loading.
- **PyTorch Lightning**: A lightweight wrapper for organizing PyTorch code, simplifying the training loop and experiment management.

Use Cases

1. Image Classification

PyTorch excels in image classification tasks, with its robust support for convolutional neural networks (CNNs). Researchers can easily build and experiment with complex architectures, achieving state-of-the-art results on benchmark datasets like CIFAR-10 and ImageNet.

2. Natural Language Processing

With the integration of libraries like TorchText, PyTorch is well-suited for NLP tasks. It supports recurrent neural networks (RNNs), transformers, and other architectures essential for tasks such as sentiment analysis, translation, and text summarization.

3. Reinforcement Learning

PyTorch is widely used in reinforcement learning due to its dynamic computation graph capabilities. Researchers can implement and test algorithms such as Q-learning, policy gradients, and actor-critic methods in a flexible environment.

4. Generative Models

With libraries like PyTorch GAN, researchers can easily implement generative adversarial networks (GANs) for tasks such as image generation and style transfer. PyTorch's flexibility makes experimenting with different architectures straightforward.

5. Time Series Analysis

PyTorch is effective for modeling time series data using LSTM and GRU networks. Applications include stock price prediction, anomaly detection, and forecasting, where sequential data modeling is crucial.

Conclusion

PyTorch has transformed the landscape of machine learning and deep learning with its dynamic computation graph, intuitive design, and extensive ecosystem. Its flexibility and ease of use make it a preferred choice for researchers and practitioners alike. As the framework continues to evolve, it empowers users to tackle complex ML challenges, innovate, and push the boundaries of artificial intelligence.

In summary, whether you are a newcomer to machine learning or an experienced researcher, PyTorch provides the tools and resources necessary to develop, train, and deploy state-of-the-art models effectively. Its strong community support, combined with ongoing developments, ensures that PyTorch remains a vital asset in the field of artificial intelligence.

Scikit-learn: A Comprehensive Overview

Introduction to Scikit-learn

Scikit-learn is an open-source machine learning library for Python that provides a wide range of tools for data analysis and modeling. Launched in 2007, it has since become one of the most widely used libraries for traditional machine learning algorithms, offering simple and efficient tools for predictive data analysis. Scikit-learn is built on top of other foundational libraries like NumPy, SciPy, and Matplotlib, making it a versatile choice for both beginners and experienced practitioners.

Key Features of Scikit-learn

1. **Wide Range of Algorithms**: Scikit-learn provides implementations of various algorithms for classification, regression, clustering, dimensionality reduction, and more.

2. **User-Friendly API**: The library offers a consistent and easy-to-use interface, allowing users to quickly build, evaluate, and refine machine learning models.

3. **Built-in Data Preprocessing**: Scikit-learn includes tools for data preprocessing, feature selection, and model evaluation, streamlining the workflow.

4. **Integration with Other Libraries**: Being built on NumPy and SciPy, Scikit-learn easily integrates with other data manipulation and visualization libraries in the Python ecosystem.

Core Components of Scikit-learn

1. Estimators

In Scikit-learn, all models are represented as estimators, which are objects that implement the methods fit(), predict(), and score(). The fit method trains the model, predict generates predictions based on the input data, and score evaluates the model's performance.

2. Pipelines

Pipelines are a way to streamline the machine learning workflow by bundling together a series of transformations and a final estimator. This helps in managing complex workflows and ensures that the same preprocessing steps are applied to both training and testing data.

Example of a simple pipeline:

python

 code

```
from sklearn.pipeline import Pipeline

from sklearn.preprocessing import StandardScaler

from sklearn.linear_model import LogisticRegression


pipeline = Pipeline([
   ('scaler', StandardScaler()),
   ('classifier', LogisticRegression())
])
```

3. Transformers and Preprocessors

Scikit-learn includes a variety of transformers and preprocessing techniques to prepare data for modeling. These include:

- **StandardScaler**: Standardizes features by removing the mean and scaling to unit variance.
- **MinMaxScaler**: Scales features to a given range, typically [0, 1].
- **OneHotEncoder**: Converts categorical variables into a format that can be provided to machine learning algorithms.

4. Model Selection and Evaluation

Scikit-learn provides tools for model selection, including cross-validation and hyperparameter tuning. Key functions include:

- **train_test_split**: Splits the dataset into training and testing subsets.
- **cross_val_score**: Evaluates a model's performance using cross-validation.
- **GridSearchCV**: Searches for the best hyperparameters by exhaustively evaluating combinations.

Types of Machine Learning Algorithms in Scikit-learn

1. Classification

Classification is the task of predicting a discrete label or category. Scikit-learn supports a wide range of classification algorithms, including:

- **Logistic Regression**: A linear model for binary classification.
- **Support Vector Machines (SVM)**: Effective in high-dimensional spaces, particularly useful for text classification.
- **Decision Trees**: A non-linear model that splits data based on feature values.
- **Random Forests**: An ensemble method that builds multiple decision trees and averages their predictions.

Example of Logistic Regression

python

code

```python
from sklearn.datasets import load_iris
from sklearn.model_selection import train_test_split
from sklearn.linear_model import LogisticRegression
from sklearn.metrics import accuracy_score

# Load dataset
data = load_iris()
X = data.data
y = data.target

# Split data
X_train, X_test, y_train, y_test = train_test_split(X, y, test_size=0.2, random_state=42)

# Train model
model = LogisticRegression()
model.fit(X_train, y_train)

# Make predictions
y_pred = model.predict(X_test)
```

```
# Evaluate model
accuracy = accuracy_score(y_test, y_pred)
print(f'Accuracy: {accuracy:.2f}')
```

2. Regression

Regression is used for predicting continuous values. Scikit-learn provides various regression algorithms, including:

- **Linear Regression**: Models the relationship between dependent and independent variables using a linear equation.
- **Ridge Regression**: A linear regression model that includes L2 regularization.
- **Lasso Regression**: A linear regression model that includes L1 regularization, useful for feature selection.
- **Support Vector Regression (SVR)**: Uses SVM principles for regression tasks.

Example of Linear Regression

python

 code

```python
from sklearn.datasets import load_boston
from sklearn.linear_model import LinearRegression
from sklearn.model_selection import train_test_split
from sklearn.metrics import mean_squared_error

# Load dataset
data = load_boston()
X = data.data
y = data.target

# Split data
X_train, X_test, y_train, y_test = train_test_split(X, y, test_size=0.2, random_state=42)

# Train model
model = LinearRegression()
model.fit(X_train, y_train)
```

```
# Make predictions
y_pred = model.predict(X_test)

# Evaluate model
mse = mean_squared_error(y_test, y_pred)
print(f'Mean Squared Error: {mse:.2f}')
```

3. Clustering

Clustering algorithms group data points into clusters based on similarity. Scikit-learn supports several clustering techniques, including:

- **K-Means**: A popular algorithm that partitions data into K clusters based on distance.
- **DBSCAN**: A density-based clustering algorithm that can identify clusters of varying shapes.
- **Agglomerative Clustering**: A hierarchical clustering method that builds clusters by merging or splitting them.

Example of K-Means Clustering

python

 code

```
from sklearn.datasets import load_iris
from sklearn.cluster import KMeans
import matplotlib.pyplot as plt

# Load dataset
data = load_iris()
X = data.data

# Train model
kmeans = KMeans(n_clusters=3)
kmeans.fit(X)

# Plot results
```

```
plt.scatter(X[:, 0], X[:, 1], c=kmeans.labels_)
plt.title('K-Means Clustering')
plt.xlabel('Feature 1')
plt.ylabel('Feature 2')
plt.show()
```

4. Dimensionality Reduction

Dimensionality reduction techniques are used to reduce the number of features in a dataset while preserving as much information as possible. Common techniques include:

- **Principal Component Analysis (PCA)**: A linear technique that transforms the data into a lower-dimensional space.
- **t-distributed Stochastic Neighbor Embedding (t-SNE)**: A non-linear technique useful for visualizing high-dimensional data.

Example of PCA

python

 code

```python
from sklearn.decomposition import PCA
from sklearn.datasets import load_iris
import matplotlib.pyplot as plt

# Load dataset
data = load_iris()
X = data.data

# Apply PCA
pca = PCA(n_components=2)
X_reduced = pca.fit_transform(X)

# Plot results
plt.scatter(X_reduced[:, 0], X_reduced[:, 1], c=data.target)
plt.title('PCA of Iris Dataset')
plt.xlabel('Principal Component 1')
```

plt.ylabel('Principal Component 2')

plt.show()

Model Evaluation and Validation

Evaluating and validating models is crucial to ensure their effectiveness. Scikit-learn offers various metrics and techniques for model evaluation:

1. Cross-Validation

Cross-validation is a technique to assess how a model generalizes to an independent dataset. The most common method is k-fold cross-validation, where the dataset is split into k subsets, and the model is trained k times, each time using a different subset for validation.

python

 code

```
from sklearn.model_selection import cross_val_score
from sklearn.linear_model import LogisticRegression


model = LogisticRegression()
scores = cross_val_score(model, X, y, cv=5)
print(f'Cross-validated scores: {scores}')
```

2. Confusion Matrix

For classification tasks, a confusion matrix is a powerful tool for understanding model performance. It shows the true positive, true negative, false positive, and false negative rates.

python

 code

```
from sklearn.metrics import confusion_matrix
import seaborn as sns


y_true = [0, 1, 0, 1]
y_pred = [0, 0, 1, 1]
cm = confusion_matrix(y_true, y_pred)


sns.heatmap(cm, annot=True, fmt='d', cmap='Blues')
plt.xlabel('Predicted')
plt.ylabel('True')
```

plt.title('Confusion Matrix')

plt.show()

3. ROC Curve and AUC

The Receiver Operating Characteristic (ROC) curve is a graphical representation of a classifier's performance at different thresholds. The Area Under the Curve (AUC) provides a single measure of performance.

python

 code

```
from sklearn.metrics import roc_curve, auc

y_scores = model.predict_proba(X_test)[:, 1]
fpr, tpr, _ = roc_curve(y_test, y_scores)
roc_auc = auc(fpr, tpr)

plt.plot(fpr, tpr, label=f'AUC = {roc_auc:.2f}')
plt.xlabel('False Positive Rate')
plt.ylabel('True Positive Rate')
plt.title('ROC Curve')
plt.legend()
plt.show()
```

Hyperparameter Tuning

Hyperparameter tuning is essential for optimizing model performance. Scikit-learn provides several methods for hyperparameter tuning:

1. Grid Search

Grid search exhaustively tests a range of hyperparameter values to find the best combination.

python

 code

```
from sklearn.model_selection import GridSearchCV

param_grid = {
    'C': [0.1, 1, 10],
```

```
    'penalty': ['l2', 'l1']
}
grid_search = GridSearchCV(LogisticRegression(), param_grid, cv=5)

grid_search.fit(X_train, y_train)

print(f'Best parameters: {grid_search.best_params_}')
```

2. Random Search

Random search samples a fixed number of hyperparameter combinations from a specified distribution, offering a faster alternative to grid search.

python

 code

```
from sklearn.model_selection import RandomizedSearchCV

random_search = RandomizedSearchCV(LogisticRegression(), param_distributions=param_grid, n_iter=10, cv=5)

random_search.fit(X_train, y_train)

print(f'Best parameters: {random_search.best_params_}')
```

Real-World Applications

Scikit-learn is used in various domains due to its versatility and ease of use. Some common applications include:

1. Finance

In finance, Scikit-learn can be used for credit scoring, fraud detection, and stock price prediction. Regression models are particularly useful for predicting numerical outcomes, while classification models can help in risk assessment.

2. Healthcare

Scikit-learn is employed in healthcare for predictive modeling, such as disease diagnosis, patient outcome prediction, and treatment efficacy analysis. Classification algorithms can assist in early disease detection based on patient data.

3. Marketing

In marketing, Scikit-learn helps in customer segmentation, churn prediction, and recommendation systems. Clustering techniques are used to group customers based on behavior, while classification models can predict customer retention.

4. Natural Language Processing

While specialized libraries like NLTK and SpaCy are often used for NLP, Scikit-learn can handle text classification, sentiment analysis, and topic modeling through vectorization techniques and traditional classifiers.

Conclusion

Scikit-learn is a powerful and versatile library for traditional machine learning. Its user-friendly interface, comprehensive documentation, and robust set of algorithms make it a go-to choice for data scientists and machine learning practitioners. Whether you are building simple models or developing complex systems, Scikit-learn provides the tools and resources necessary to streamline your workflow and achieve your objectives.

From classification to regression, clustering to dimensionality reduction, Scikit-learn covers a wide array of machine learning tasks, making it a fundamental library in the Python ecosystem. As machine learning continues to evolve, Scikit-learn remains an essential toolkit for tackling a variety of data analysis challenges, ensuring that users can build effective models efficiently and effectively.

Keras: A Comprehensive Overview

Introduction to Keras

Keras is an open-source high-level neural networks API, designed to simplify the process of building and training deep learning models. Initially developed by François Chollet in 2015, Keras has become one of the most popular frameworks for deep learning, particularly due to its user-friendly interface and ability to run on top of TensorFlow, Theano, or Microsoft Cognitive Toolkit (CNTK). In 2017, Keras was integrated into TensorFlow as tf.keras, making it the official high-level API for TensorFlow.

Key Features of Keras

1. **User-Friendly API**: Keras emphasizes simplicity and ease of use, allowing users to build complex neural networks with -mal code.

2. **Modular and Composable**: Keras models are constructed as a series of layers and operations, making it easy to modify and extend models.

3. **Support for Multiple Backends**: While tightly integrated with TensorFlow, Keras also supports other backends, providing flexibility in terms of computational resources.

4. **Pre-trained Models**: Keras includes a variety of pre-trained models for common tasks, allowing users to leverage transfer learning effectively.

5. **Extensive Documentation and Community**: Keras has a strong community and comprehensive documentation, making it accessible for both beginners and experienced practitioners.

Core Components of Keras

1. Models

Keras provides two main ways to create models: the Sequential API and the Functional API.

Sequential API

The Sequential API is a linear stack of layers. It is straightforward and easy to use for building simple models.

python

 code

```
from keras.models import Sequential
from keras.layers import Dense

model = Sequential()
model.add(Dense(64, activation='relu', input_shape=(32,)))  # Input layer
model.add(Dense(10, activation='softmax'))  # Output layer
```

Functional API

The Functional API offers greater flexibility, allowing for the creation of complex architectures such as multi-input or multi-output models.

python

 code

```
from keras.layers import Input, Dense
from keras.models import Model

inputs = Input(shape=(32,))
x = Dense(64, activation='relu')(inputs)
outputs = Dense(10, activation='softmax')(x)

model = Model(inputs=inputs, outputs=outputs)
```

2. Layers

Keras provides a wide variety of layers to build neural networks, including:

- **Dense**: Fully connected layer.
- **Conv2D**: Convolutional layer for 2D input (e.g., images).
- **MaxPooling2D**: Max pooling layer to down-sample feature maps.
- **LSTM**: Long Short-Term Memory layer for sequence data.
- **Dropout**: Regularization layer to prevent overfitting.

3. Activation Functions

Keras supports several activation functions that introduce non-linearity into models:
- **ReLU**: Rectified Linear Unit, commonly used in hidden layers.
- **Sigmoid**: Used in binary classification tasks.
- **Softmax**: Used in multi-class classification problems.

4. Loss Functions

Keras includes various loss functions to measure model performance during training:
- **Binary Crossentropy**: Used for binary classification.
- **Categorical Crossentropy**: Used for multi-class classification.
- **Mean Squared Error**: Used for regression tasks.

5. Optimizers

Keras supports a range of optimization algorithms for training models, such as:
- **SGD**: Stochastic Gradient Descent.
- **Adam**: Adaptive Moment Estimation, widely used for its efficiency.
- **RMSprop**: Designed for non-stationary objectives.

Building a Model with Keras

Step 1: Data Preparation

Before building a model, it's essential to prepare the data. This often includes loading datasets, splitting them into training and testing sets, and performing any necessary preprocessing (e.g., normalization, encoding categorical variables).

python

code

```python
from sklearn.model_selection import train_test_split
from sklearn.datasets import load_iris
import numpy as np

# Load dataset
data = load_iris()
X = data.data
y = data.target

# One-hot encode labels
```

y = np.eye(3)[y] # Assuming 3 classes

Split data

X_train, X_test, y_train, y_test = train_test_split(X, y, test_size=0.2, random_state=42)

Step 2: Model Creation

Using the Sequential API, a simple model can be created as follows:

python

 code

model = Sequential()

model.add(Dense(64, activation='relu', input_shape=(4,))) # Input layer for 4 features

model.add(Dense(3, activation='softmax')) # Output layer for 3 classes

Step 3: Compiling the Model

Before training the model, it must be compiled with a chosen optimizer, loss function, and evaluation metric.

python

 code

model.compile(optimizer='adam',

      loss='categorical_crossentropy',

      metrics=['accuracy'])

Step 4: Training the Model

The model can be trained using the fit() method, which allows for specifying epochs, batch size, and validation data.

python

 code

history = model.fit(X_train, y_train,

      epochs=100,

      batch_size=5,

      validation_data=(X_test, y_test))

Step 5: Evaluating the Model

Once the model is trained, its performance can be evaluated on the test set using the evaluate() method.

```python
loss, accuracy = model.evaluate(X_test, y_test)
print(f'Test accuracy: {accuracy:.2f}')
```

Step 6: Making Predictions

Predictions can be made using the predict() method.

```python
predictions = model.predict(X_test)
predicted_classes = np.argmax(predictions, axis=1)
```

Advanced Features of Keras

1. Callbacks

Callbacks are functions that can be applied at different stages of training, such as after each epoch. Keras includes several built-in callbacks, like EarlyStopping, which stops training when a monitored metric has stopped improving, and ModelCheckpoint, which saves the model after every epoch.

```python
from keras.callbacks import EarlyStopping, ModelCheckpoint

early_stopping = EarlyStopping(monitor='val_loss', patience=10)
model_checkpoint = ModelCheckpoint('best_model.h5', save_best_only=True)

model.fit(X_train, y_train,
        epochs=100,
        validation_data=(X_test, y_test),
        callbacks=[early_stopping, model_checkpoint])
```

2. Transfer Learning

Keras makes it easy to use pre-trained models for transfer learning. You can leverage models like VGG16, ResNet, or InceptionV3 for tasks like image classification. The pre-trained model can be fine-tuned on a new dataset by freezing certain layers and training the rest.

python

```
code
from keras.applications import VGG16

base_model = VGG16(weights='imagenet', include_top=False, input_shape=(224, 224, 3))
for layer in base_model.layers:
    layer.trainable = False  # Freeze layers

# Add custom layers for your specific task
```

3. Custom Loss Functions and Metrics

Keras allows you to define custom loss functions and metrics if the built-in ones do not fit your needs. This flexibility is useful for specialized tasks.

python

```
code
import keras.backend as K

def custom_loss(y_true, y_pred):
    return K.mean(K.square(y_pred - y_true), axis=-1)

model.compile(optimizer='adam', loss=custom_loss)
```

4. Regularization Techniques

Regularization methods such as Dropout and L2 regularization can be easily integrated into Keras models to prevent overfitting.

python

```
code
from keras.layers import Dropout

model.add(Dropout(0.5))  # 50% dropout rate
```

5. Batch Normalization

Batch normalization can be applied to stabilize and accelerate training. It normalizes the output of a previous activation layer by subtracting the batch mean and dividing by the batch standard deviation.

python

code

from keras.layers import BatchNormalization

model.add(BatchNormalization())

Real-World Applications of Keras

1. Computer Vision

Keras is widely used for image classification, object detection, and segmentation tasks. Its ease of use and support for convolutional neural networks (CNNs) make it a go-to choice for computer vision applications.

2. Natural Language Processing

Keras is used in various NLP tasks such as text classification, sentiment analysis, and language translation. Recurrent neural networks (RNNs) and LSTM layers facilitate modeling sequential data effectively.

3. Time Series Forecasting

Keras can model time series data using RNNs or LSTMs to predict future values based on past observations, applicable in finance, weather forecasting, and inventory management.

4. Reinforcement Learning

While Keras is primarily designed for supervised learning tasks, it can also be used in reinforcement learning scenarios, particularly in conjunction with libraries like TensorFlow and OpenAI Gym.

5. Healthcare

Keras is applied in medical imaging, such as classifying X-ray or MRI images, predicting patient outcomes, and assisting in diagnostics based on patient data.

Conclusion

Keras stands out as a powerful and user-friendly high-level API for building neural networks, making it an essential tool for both beginners and experienced data scientists. Its seamless integration with TensorFlow allows for robust model development and deployment, while its wide range of features, from simple model creation to complex custom architectures, caters to various deep learning applications.

With extensive documentation, a supportive community, and ongoing developments, Keras continues to evolve as a key player in the machine learning landscape. Whether you are tackling simple classification tasks or complex neural architectures, Keras provides the flexibility and functionality necessary to succeed in your deep learning projects.

Pandas: A Comprehensive Overview for Data Manipulation and Analysis

Introduction to Pandas

Pandas is an open-source Python library that provides powerful data manipulation and analysis tools, primarily designed for structured data. Developed by Wes McKinney in 2008, Pandas has become an essential library for data scientists and analysts, enabling them to work efficiently with large datasets. The library's primary data structures, Series and DataFrame, allow for intuitive data handling, making it easier to clean, transform, and analyze data.

Key Features of Pandas

1. **Data Structures**: Pandas introduces two main data structures—Series (1-dimensional) and DataFrame (2-dimensional)—that facilitate data manipulation.

2. **Flexible Data Handling**: Supports heterogeneous data types, enabling users to store different types of data within the same structure.

3. **Data Alignment**: Automatically aligns data for operations based on index, simplifying data manipulation tasks.

4. **Robust I/O Capabilities**: Easily read from and write to various file formats, including CSV, Excel, SQL databases, and JSON.

5. **Powerful Data Analysis Tools**: Provides tools for data aggregation, grouping, filtering, and statistical analysis.
6. **Time Series Functionality**: Excellent support for working with time series data, including date and time indexing.

Core Components of Pandas

1. Data Structures

Series

A Pandas Series is a one-dimensional labeled array that can hold any data type. It is similar to a list or array but comes with additional capabilities, such as labels for each element.

python

 code

```python
import pandas as pd

# Creating a Series
data = pd.Series([1, 2, 3, 4], index=['a', 'b', 'c', 'd'])
print(data)
```

DataFrame

A DataFrame is a two-dimensional labeled data structure that consists of rows and columns. It is akin to a spreadsheet or SQL table, making it versatile for various data manipulation tasks.

python

 code

```python
# Creating a DataFrame
data = {
    'Name': ['Alice', 'Bob', 'Charlie'],
    'Age': [25, 30, 35],
    'City': ['New York', 'Los Angeles', 'Chicago']
}
df = pd.DataFrame(data)
print(df)
```

2. Reading and Writing Data

Pandas provides functions to read from and write to various data formats:

- **CSV Files**: Read and write data in CSV format.
- **Excel Files**: Read from and write to Excel spreadsheets.
- **SQL Databases**: Connect to SQL databases to execute queries and retrieve data.

python

 code

```python
# Reading a CSV file
df = pd.read_csv('data.csv')

# Writing to an Excel file
df.to_excel('output.xlsx', index=False)
```

3. Data Exploration

Inspecting Data

Pandas offers several functions to inspect data quickly, including:

- head(): Displays the first few rows of the DataFrame.
- info(): Provides a concise summary of the DataFrame, including data types and non-null counts.
- describe(): Generates descriptive statistics of the DataFrame's numeric columns.

python

 code

```python
print(df.head())
print(df.info())
print(df.describe())
```

4. Data Manipulation

Selecting and Filtering Data

Pandas allows for flexible selection and filtering of data using labels, indices, or boolean conditions.

python

 code

```python
# Selecting a column
ages = df['Age']
```

```
# Filtering rows based on a condition
adults = df[df['Age'] >= 30]
```

Modifying Data

You can easily modify DataFrame values, add new columns, or drop existing ones.

python

 code

```
# Adding a new column
df['Salary'] = [70000, 80000, 90000]


# Dropping a column
df.drop('City', axis=1, inplace=True)
```

Handling Missing Data

Pandas provides tools for detecting and handling missing data:

- **Detecting Missing Values**: Use isnull() to identify missing values.
- **Filling Missing Values**: Use fillna() to fill missing values with a specified value or method.
- **Dropping Missing Values**: Use dropna() to remove rows or columns with missing values.

python

 code

```
df['Age'].fillna(df['Age'].mean(), inplace=True)  # Fill with mean age
df.dropna(inplace=True)  # Drop any rows with missing values
```

5. Grouping and Aggregating Data

Pandas makes it easy to group data and perform aggregation functions:

python

 code

```
# Grouping by a column and calculating the mean
grouped = df.groupby('City').mean()


# Aggregating with multiple functions
agg_result = df.groupby('City').agg({'Age': ['mean', 'min'], 'Salary': 'sum'})
```

6. Merging and Joining DataFrames

Pandas allows you to combine multiple DataFrames using merge and join operations, similar to SQL joins.

python

 code

```
df1 = pd.DataFrame({'Key': ['A', 'B', 'C'], 'Value1': [1, 2, 3]})
df2 = pd.DataFrame({'Key': ['B', 'C', 'D'], 'Value2': [4, 5, 6]})

# Merging DataFrames
merged_df = pd.merge(df1, df2, on='Key', how='inner')  # Inner join
```

7. Time Series Analysis

Pandas offers extensive functionality for working with time series data, including:

- **Date and Time Indexing**: Create time series data with a date index.
- **Resampling**: Change the frequency of time series data.
- **Rolling Windows**: Apply functions over a rolling window for moving averages and other calculations.

python

 code

```
# Creating a time series
dates = pd.date_range(start='2022-01-01', periods=5, freq='D')
data = pd.Series([1, 2, 3, 4, 5], index=dates)

# Resampling the time series
resampled = data.resample('2D').sum()  # Sum every 2 days
```

8. Data Visualization

While Pandas does not directly include visualization tools, it integrates well with libraries like Matplotlib and Seaborn to create visualizations.

python

 code

```
import matplotlib.pyplot as plt
```

```
# Simple line plot
data.plot(title='Sample Data')
plt.show()
```

Real-World Applications of Pandas

1. Data Cleaning and Preparation

Pandas is often the first step in data analysis, helping analysts clean and prepare raw data for further analysis or modeling.

2. Exploratory Data Analysis (EDA)

Data scientists use Pandas for exploratory analysis to uncover trends, patterns, and insights from datasets.

3. Financial Analysis

Pandas is widely used in finance for analyzing time series data, performing portfolio analysis, and backtesting trading strategies.

4. Machine Learning Preprocessing

Pandas helps in preprocessing data for machine learning, such as handling missing values, encoding categorical variables, and feature selection.

5. Web Scraping and Data Acquisition

Pandas can be used to gather data from APIs or scrape web data, facilitating the creation of datasets for analysis.

Conclusion

Pandas is an essential library for data manipulation and analysis in Python. Its powerful data structures, flexible handling of different data types, and robust functionalities make it an invaluable tool for data scientists and analysts. Whether you are cleaning data, performing exploratory analysis, or preparing datasets for machine learning, Pandas provides the capabilities needed to work efficiently and effectively.

With its extensive documentation and supportive community, mastering Pandas is a vital step for anyone looking to excel in data analysis and manipulation. Whether you are a beginner or an experienced practitioner, Pandas can significantly enhance your data handling capabilities and streamline your workflow.

NumPy: A Comprehensive Overview

Introduction to NumPy

NumPy (Numerical Python) is an open-source library in Python that provides support for large, multi-dimensional arrays and matrices, along with a collection of mathematical functions to operate on these arrays. Developed in the early 2000s, NumPy has become a fundamental library for scientific computing and data analysis in Python, serving as the backbone for many other libraries, including Pandas, SciPy, and TensorFlow.

Key Features of NumPy

1. **N-Dimensional Arrays**: NumPy's primary feature is its powerful N-dimensional array object, known as ndarray, which enables efficient storage and manipulation of large datasets.

2. **Broadcasting**: A powerful mechanism that allows NumPy to perform operations on arrays of different shapes, enabling more flexible and efficient computations.
3. **Mathematical Functions**: A rich library of mathematical functions for performing element-wise operations, statistical analysis, and linear algebra.
4. **Performance**: NumPy is implemented in C, allowing for significant performance improvements over pure code, especially for large datasets.
5. **Interoperability**: Works well with other libraries and languages, making it a versatile choice for various scientific and data analysis tasks.

Core Components of NumPy

1. N-Dimensional Arrays

The core data structure in NumPy is the ndarray, which is a fast and flexible container for large data sets in Python. Arrays can be created from lists, tuples, or other arrays.

python

code

```
import numpy as np

# Creating a 1D array
array_1d = np.array([1, 2, 3, 4])

# Creating a 2D array (matrix)
array_2d = np.array([[1, 2, 3], [4, 5, 6]])

print(array_1d)
print(array_2d)
```

2. Array Properties

NumPy arrays come with several important attributes that describe their properties:

- **Shape**: The dimensions of the array.
- **Data Type**: The type of elements stored in the array.
- **Size**: The total number of elements in the array.

python

code

```
print(array_2d.shape)  # Output: (2, 3)
```

```
print(array_2d.dtype)  # Output: int64 (or another type based on the data)
print(array_2d.size)   # Output: 6
```

3. Array Indexing and Slicing

NumPy supports advanced indexing and slicing, allowing for flexible access to array elements.

python

code

```
# Accessing elements
element = array_2d[0, 1]  # Accessing the element at row 0, column 1

# Slicing arrays
slice_array = array_2d[:, 1]  # Accessing all rows, column 1
```

4. Array Operations

NumPy enables element-wise operations and mathematical computations efficiently:

- **Arithmetic Operations**: Perform addition, subtraction, multiplication, and division directly on arrays.

python

code

```
array_a = np.array([1, 2, 3])
array_b = np.array([4, 5, 6])

result_add = array_a + array_b
result_mul = array_a * array_b
```

- **Mathematical Functions**: Functions like np.sum(), np.mean(), np.max(), and np.min() can be applied directly to arrays.

python

code

```
mean_value = np.mean(array_a)  # Calculate mean
sum_value = np.sum(array_b)    # Calculate sum
```

5. Broadcasting

Broadcasting is a powerful feature that allows NumPy to perform arithmetic operations on arrays of different shapes.

python

 code

array_c = np.array([[1], [2], [3]])

array_d = np.array([4, 5, 6])

result_broadcast = array_c + array_d # Broadcasting allows addition

6. Reshaping and Resizing

NumPy provides methods to reshape and resize arrays without changing the data.

python

 code

array_reshaped = array_2d.reshape(3, 2) # Reshaping to 3 rows, 2 columns

7. Linear Algebra

NumPy includes functions for linear algebra operations, such as matrix multiplication, determinants, and eigenvalues.

python

 code

Matrix multiplication

matrix_a = np.array([[1, 2], [3, 4]])

matrix_b = np.array([[5, 6], [7, 8]])

product = np.dot(matrix_a, matrix_b)

Computing the determinant

determinant = np.linalg.det(matrix_a)

8. Random Number Generation

NumPy has a built-in random module for generating random numbers, which is useful for simulations and statistical modeling.

python

 code

Generate random numbers

random_array = np.random.rand(3, 2) # 3x2 array of random floats in [0, 1)

Real-World Applications of NumPy

1. Scientific Computing

NumPy is widely used in scientific computing, providing a solid foundation for various scientific applications, including simulations, modeling, and numerical analysis.

2. Data Analysis

As a foundational library for data manipulation, NumPy is often used in conjunction with libraries like Pandas to perform efficient data analysis.

3. Machine Learning

Many machine learning libraries, such as TensorFlow and Scikit-learn, rely on NumPy for numerical operations. It serves as the backbone for handling data in ML models.

4. Financial Analysis

NumPy is employed in quantitative finance for tasks such as portfolio optimization, risk management, and option pricing.

5. Image Processing

In image processing, NumPy arrays are used to represent images as multi-dimensional arrays, allowing for efficient manipulation and analysis of pixel data.

Conclusion

NumPy is an essential library for anyone working with numerical data in Python. Its powerful array structure, efficient performance, and extensive mathematical capabilities make it the go-to choice for scientific computing and data analysis. Whether you are cleaning data, performing complex mathematical computations, or building machine learning models, NumPy provides the tools necessary to streamline your workflow.

With a strong community and comprehensive documentation, mastering NumPy is a crucial step for anyone looking to excel in data science, machine learning, or scientific research. Its foundational role in the Python ecosystem ensures that NumPy will remain a key player in numerical computing for years to come.

Dask:

A Comprehensive Overview for Parallel Computing and Large Datasets

Introduction to Dask

Dask is an open-source parallel computing library in Python designed for handling large datasets and performing computations that do not fit into memory. It provides advanced parallelism for analytics and enables users to scale their computations from single machines to distributed clusters seamlessly. Dask's design allows it to integrate well with existing Python data science libraries like NumPy, Pandas, and Scikit-learn, making it a versatile tool for data analysis.

Key Features of Dask

1. **Dynamic Task Scheduling**: Dask uses a dynamic task scheduler that builds a task graph on-the-fly, allowing for flexible execution of complex workflows.

2. **Parallel Collections**: Dask provides parallelized versions of standard Python data structures, such as arrays, dataframes, and bags, enabling users to work with larger-than-memory datasets.

3. **Familiar APIs**: Dask's API is similar to those of NumPy and Pandas, making it easy for users familiar with these libraries to adopt Dask without a steep learning curve.

4. **Scalability**: Dask can scale computations from a single machine to a large cluster, handling both distributed and multi-threaded execution.

5. **Integration with Other Libraries**: Dask works seamlessly with other Python libraries, allowing for powerful data manipulation and analysis.

Core Components of Dask

1. Dask Arrays

Dask Arrays are parallelized versions of NumPy arrays that enable operations on large datasets that do not fit into memory. They are built on top of NumPy, maintaining a similar interface.

python

 code

import dask.array as da

Create a large Dask array

x = da.random.random(size=(10000, 10000), chunks=(1000, 1000))

print(x)

2. Dask DataFrames

Dask DataFrames are similar to Pandas DataFrames but are designed to operate on larger-than-memory datasets. They break data into smaller partitions, allowing for parallel computation.

python

 code

import dask.dataframe as dd

Create a Dask DataFrame from a CSV file

df = dd.read_csv('large_dataset.csv')

print(df.head())

3. Dask Bags

Dask Bags are designed for handling semi-structured or unstructured data, similar to Python lists. They provide a parallelized approach to processing collections of Python objects.

python

 code

import dask.bag as db

Create a Dask Bag

bag = db.from_sequence(['Alice', 'Bob', 'Charlie'], npartitions=2)

print(bag.map(lambda x: x.upper()).compute())

4. Task Scheduling and Execution

Dask constructs a task graph, representing the series of operations to perform. The compute() method triggers the execution of the entire graph, distributing the work across available resources.

python

 code

Compute the result

result = df['column_name'].mean().compute()

print(result)

5. Delayed Execution

Dask supports lazy evaluation, allowing you to define a sequence of operations without executing them immediately. This can improve performance by optimizing the execution plan.

python

 code

from dask import delayed

@delayed

def process_data(data):

   # Data processing steps

   return processed_data

Create a delayed computation

result = process_data(df).compute()

Use Cases for Dask

1. Big Data Processing

Dask is well-suited for big data applications, allowing users to work with datasets that exceed the memory limits of their hardware. It handles data chunking and processing efficiently.

2. Parallel Computing

With Dask, users can parallelize operations, leveraging multi-core processors or distributed clusters. This is particularly useful for CPU-bound tasks such as large-scale numerical simulations.

3. Machine Learning

Dask can be integrated into machine learning workflows, enabling scalable data preprocessing, model training, and hyperparameter optimization with libraries like Scikit-learn.

4. Data Analysis and Exploration

Dask DataFrames provide a familiar API for data analysis, enabling users to perform exploratory data analysis on large datasets without requiring significant changes to their workflow.

5. Real-Time Data Processing

Dask can handle streaming data and real-time processing, making it suitable for applications that require immediate analysis of incoming data streams.

Real-World Applications of Dask

1. Financial Services

Dask is often used in financial analysis for processing large datasets related to transactions, market data, and risk assessments, enabling efficient analysis and modeling.

2. Genomics

In bioinformatics, Dask can handle large genomic datasets, supporting tasks like sequence analysis, variant calling, and population studies.

3. Climate Science

Dask is employed in climate modeling and analysis, where researchers need to process vast amounts of data generated by simulations and observations.

4. E-Commerce

Dask can analyze customer behavior and sales data in e-commerce applications, enabling real-time insights and recommendations.

Conclusion

Dask is a powerful library for parallel computing and managing large datasets in Python. Its dynamic task scheduling, familiar API, and scalability make it an essential tool for data scientists and engineers working with big data. Whether you are processing large datasets, performing complex computations, or building machine learning models, Dask provides the flexibility and efficiency needed to tackle these challenges.

With its strong integration with other Python libraries and an active community, Dask continues to evolve, making it a vital component of the data science ecosystem. Mastering Dask opens up new possibilities for working with data, allowing for more efficient and scalable analysis in various domains.

Matplotlib: A Comprehensive Overview for Data Visualization

Introduction to Matplotlib

Matplotlib is a widely-used, open-source plotting library in Python that provides a flexible way to create static, interactive, and animated visualizations. Developed by John D. Hunter in 2003, it has become one of the foundational libraries for data visualization in the Python ecosystem. With its extensive capabilities, Matplotlib allows users to create a wide range of visual representations, from simple line plots to complex 3D visualizations.

Key Features of Matplotlib

1. **Versatile Plot Types**: Matplotlib supports a wide variety of plot types, including line plots, scatter plots, bar charts, histograms, and more.

2. **Customizability**: It offers extensive options for customizing visual elements, such as colors, labels, and markers, allowing users to create tailored visualizations.

3. **Integration with NumPy and Pandas**: Matplotlib works seamlessly with NumPy arrays and Pandas DataFrames, making it easy to plot data directly from these structures.

4. **Interactive Plots**: Supports interactive features, enabling users to zoom, pan, and update visualizations dynamically.

5. **Subplots and Multiple Figures**: Users can create complex layouts with multiple plots in a single figure using subplots.

Core Components of Matplotlib

1. Basic Plotting

Creating a basic plot with Matplotlib involves a few simple steps: importing the library, preparing the data, and using the plot() function.

python

 code

```
import matplotlib.pyplot as plt

# Sample data
x = [1, 2, 3, 4, 5]
y = [2, 3, 5, 7, 11]

# Creating a simple line plot
plt.plot(x, y)
plt.title("Simple Line Plot")
plt.xlabel("X-axis")
plt.ylabel("Y-axis")
plt.show()
```

2. Customizing Plots

Matplotlib provides extensive options for customizing plots. You can change colors, line styles, markers, and add annotations.

python

 code

```
plt.plot(x, y, color='red', linestyle='--', marker='o')
plt.title("Customized Line Plot")
plt.xlabel("X-axis")
plt.ylabel("Y-axis")
plt.grid(True)
plt.annotate("Point (3, 5)", xy=(3, 5), xytext=(4, 6), arrowprops=dict(arrowstyle='->'))
plt.show()
```

3. Creating Different Plot Types

Matplotlib supports various plot types, each suited for different kinds of data and insights.

Bar Charts

Bar charts are useful for comparing quantities across categories.

python

 code

```
categories = ['A', 'B', 'C']
values = [3, 7, 5]

plt.bar(categories, values, color='blue')
plt.title("Bar Chart Example")
plt.ylabel("Values")
plt.show()
```

Histograms

Histograms are effective for visualizing the distribution of a dataset.

python

 code

```
data = [1, 2, 2, 3, 3, 3, 4, 5, 5, 5, 5, 6]

plt.hist(data, bins=5, color='green', alpha=0.7)
plt.title("Histogram Example")
plt.xlabel("Value")
plt.ylabel("Frequency")
plt.show()
```

Scatter Plots

Scatter plots are great for showing relationships between two continuous variables.

python

 code

```
x = [1, 2, 3, 4, 5]
y = [2, 3, 5, 7, 11]
```

```python
plt.scatter(x, y, color='purple')
plt.title("Scatter Plot Example")
plt.xlabel("X-axis")
plt.ylabel("Y-axis")
plt.show()
```

4. Subplots and Layouts

Matplotlib allows you to create multiple plots in a single figure using subplots.

python

code

```
fig, axs = plt.subplots(2, 2)

# Top-left
axs[0, 0].plot(x, y, color='blue')
axs[0, 0].set_title("Plot 1")

# Top-right
axs[0, 1].bar(categories, values)
axs[0, 1].set_title("Plot 2")

# Bottom-left
axs[1, 0].hist(data)
axs[1, 0].set_title("Plot 3")

# Bottom-right
axs[1, 1].scatter(x, y)
axs[1, 1].set_title("Plot 4")

plt.tight_layout()
plt.show()
```

5. Saving Figures

You can easily save your plots to various file formats, including PNG, PDF, and SVG.

python

 code

plt.plot(x, y)

plt.title("Save This Plot")

plt.savefig('my_plot.png')

6. Interactive Plots

Matplotlib supports interactive plotting through backends like %matplotlib notebook in Jupyter Notebooks, allowing for zooming and panning.

python

 code

%matplotlib notebook

plt.plot(x, y)

plt.title("Interactive Plot")

plt.show()

7. 3D Plotting

Matplotlib also supports 3D plotting through the mpl_toolkits.mplot3d module.

python

 code

from mpl_toolkits.mplot3d import Axes3D

fig = plt.figure()

ax = fig.add_subplot(111, projection='3d')

ax.scatter(x, y, zs=[1, 2, 3, 4, 5], c='r')

ax.set_title("3D Scatter Plot")

plt.show()

Real-World Applications of Matplotlib

1. Data Analysis and Exploration

Matplotlib is extensively used for exploratory data analysis (EDA), helping data scientists visualize patterns, trends, and anomalies in data.

2. Scientific Research

Researchers in various fields utilize Matplotlib for plotting experimental data, statistical results, and simulations to communicate findings effectively.

3. Financial Analysis

In finance, Matplotlib is used to visualize stock prices, market trends, and financial indicators, aiding in decision-making processes.

4. Machine Learning

Matplotlib plays a crucial role in machine learning for visualizing model performance, feature importance, and results from experiments.

5. Education and Presentation

Matplotlib is frequently employed in educational contexts to illustrate mathematical concepts, data structures, and algorithm performance.

Conclusion

Matplotlib is a powerful and versatile library for data visualization in Python. Its ability to create a wide range of static, interactive, and animated plots makes it an invaluable tool for data scientists, researchers, and analysts. With its extensive customization options, integration with other libraries, and user-friendly API, Matplotlib enables users to convey insights effectively through visual representations.

By mastering Matplotlib, you can enhance your data analysis workflows, present data-driven findings clearly, and make informed decisions based on visual insights. Whether you are creating simple line plots or complex multi-dimensional visualizations, Matplotlib provides the tools necessary to bring your data to life.

Seaborn: A Comprehensive Overview for

Statistical Data Visualization

Introduction to Seaborn

Seaborn is an open-source Python visualization library built on top of Matplotlib that provides a high-level interface for creating attractive and informative statistical graphics. Developed by Michael Waskom, Seaborn is designed to enhance the visual appeal of plots while simplifying the process of creating complex visualizations. With its focus on statistical data visualization, Seaborn makes it easy to generate plots that help communicate data insights effectively.

Key Features of Seaborn

1. **High-Level Interface**: Seaborn simplifies the creation of complex visualizations with concise commands, making it accessible for both beginners and experienced users.

2. **Statistical Functions**: Built-in functions for performing statistical operations, such as regression, can be easily incorporated into visualizations.

3. **Thematic Styles**: Seaborn comes with several aesthetic themes and color palettes to enhance the visual appeal of plots.

4. **Integration with Pandas**: Seamless integration with Pandas DataFrames allows users to plot data directly from their data structures.

5. **Complex Visualizations Made Simple**: Functions for creating multi-plot grids and visualizing relationships between multiple variables facilitate exploratory data analysis.

Core Components of Seaborn

1. Setting Up Seaborn

To get started with Seaborn, you need to install it and import it along with Matplotlib.

bash

 code

pip install seaborn

python

 code

import seaborn as sns

import matplotlib.pyplot as plt

2. Thematic Styles and Color Palettes

Seaborn allows users to easily change the aesthetic style of plots and customize color palettes.

python

 code

```python
# Set the aesthetic style
sns.set(style="whitegrid")

# Use a built-in color palette
sns.set_palette("pastel")
```

3. Basic Plots

Scatter Plots

Seaborn makes it easy to create scatter plots with added regression lines.

python

 code

```python
# Sample data
tips = sns.load_dataset("tips")

# Create a scatter plot with a regression line
sns.scatterplot(data=tips, x="total_bill", y="tip", hue="time", style="sex")
sns.regplot(data=tips, x="total_bill", y="tip", scatter=False, color='orange')
plt.title("Scatter Plot with Regression Line")
plt.show()
```

Bar Plots

Bar plots are used to show the relationship between a categorical variable and a quantitative variable.

python

 code

```python
# Create a bar plot
sns.barplot(data=tips, x="day", y="total_bill", ci="sd", palette="Blues")
plt.title("Average Total Bill by Day")
```

plt.show()

Box Plots

Box plots are useful for visualizing the distribution of a dataset and identifying outliers.

python

 code

```
# Create a box plot
sns.boxplot(data=tips, x="day", y="total_bill", palette="Set2")
plt.title("Box Plot of Total Bills by Day")
plt.show()
```

4. Advanced Visualizations

Pair Plots

Pair plots allow for the visualization of relationships between all pairs of variables in a dataset.

python

 code

```
# Create a pair plot
sns.pairplot(tips, hue="sex")
plt.title("Pair Plot of Tips Dataset")
plt.show()
```

Heatmaps

Heatmaps are effective for visualizing correlation matrices and categorical data.

python

 code

```
# Calculate the correlation matrix
correlation = tips.corr()

# Create a heatmap
sns.heatmap(correlation, annot=True, cmap='coolwarm')
plt.title("Correlation Heatmap")
plt.show()
```

5. Customizing Plots

Seaborn allows for extensive customization of plots, including axes, titles, and labels.

python

code

```
# Create a scatter plot with customizations
plt.figure(figsize=(10, 6))
scatter = sns.scatterplot(data=tips, x="total_bill", y="tip", hue="day", style="time", s=100)
plt.title("Tips vs. Total Bill", fontsize=16)
plt.xlabel("Total Bill ($)", fontsize=14)
plt.ylabel("Tip ($)", fontsize=14)
plt.legend(title='Day and Time', loc='upper left')
plt.show()
```

6. Faceting

Seaborn's faceting capabilities allow you to create a grid of plots based on the values of a categorical variable.

python

code

```
# Create a faceted grid of scatter plots
g = sns.FacetGrid(tips, col="time", row="sex")
g.map(sns.scatterplot, "total_bill", "tip")
g.add_legend()
plt.show()
```

Real-World Applications of Seaborn

1. Exploratory Data Analysis (EDA)

Seaborn is an invaluable tool for EDA, helping data scientists visualize relationships, distributions, and trends in their datasets.

2. Statistical Analysis

With its built-in statistical functions, Seaborn facilitates visualizing regression results, distributions, and comparisons, making it ideal for statistical analysis.

3. Presentation of Results

Seaborn's aesthetic capabilities make it a preferred choice for creating publication-quality visualizations in reports, presentations, and academic papers.

4. Business Intelligence

Data analysts in business settings use Seaborn to create visualizations that support decision-making, helping stakeholders understand data trends and insights.

5. Education

Seaborn is widely used in educational contexts for teaching data visualization concepts and statistical analysis.

Conclusion

Seaborn is a powerful and user-friendly library for statistical data visualization in Python. By building on Matplotlib, it simplifies the process of creating informative and visually appealing plots. With its rich set of features, including high-level plotting functions, aesthetic themes, and integration with Pandas, Seaborn enables data scientists and analysts to explore and communicate their data insights effectively.

By mastering Seaborn, you can elevate your data visualization skills, create compelling visual narratives, and make data-driven decisions based on clear and insightful graphics. Whether you are conducting exploratory analysis, presenting findings, or communicating complex information, Seaborn provides the tools you need to succeed.

Plotly: A Comprehensive Overview for Interactive Data Visualization

Introduction to Plotly

Plotly is an open-source graphing library for Python that enables the creation of interactive plots and dashboards. It is widely used for exploratory data analysis and data visualization, allowing users to create complex visualizations that are both beautiful and informative. With its ability to produce interactive charts, Plotly enhances user engagement and data exploration, making it a powerful tool for data scientists, analysts, and developers.

Key Features of Plotly

1. **Interactivity**: Plotly charts are inherently interactive, allowing users to hover, zoom, and pan, making data exploration intuitive and engaging.
2. **Wide Range of Plot Types**: Supports a variety of chart types, including scatter plots, bar charts, line charts, heatmaps, 3D plots, and more.
3. **Dashboards**: Plotly Dash, an extension of Plotly, enables the creation of web applications and dashboards with interactive visualizations.
4. **Integration**: Seamlessly integrates with other data science libraries like Pandas and NumPy, facilitating easy data manipulation and visualization.
5. **Web-Based**: Charts can be embedded in web applications and shared easily through URLs, making it ideal for collaborative environments.

Core Components of Plotly

1. Installation

To use Plotly, you need to install it via pip:

bash

 code

```
pip install plotly
```

2. Basic Plotting

Creating a basic plot with Plotly is straightforward. You can use the plotly.express module for quick and easy visualizations.

python

 code

```
import plotly.express as px
import pandas as pd

# Sample data
df = pd.DataFrame({
    "x": [1, 2, 3, 4, 5],
    "y": [2, 3, 5, 7, 11],
    "label": ["A", "B", "C", "D", "E"]
})

# Create a simple scatter plot
```

```python
fig = px.scatter(df, x="x", y="y", text="label", title="Simple Scatter Plot")
fig.show()
```

3. Customizing Plots

Plotly allows for extensive customization of plots, from layout to color scales.

python

code

```python
# Create a customized scatter plot
fig = px.scatter(df, x="x", y="y", text="label", title="Customized Scatter Plot")
fig.update_traces(marker=dict(size=12, color='blue', line=dict(width=2, color='DarkSlateGrey')))
fig.update_layout(title_font_size=20)
fig.show()
```

4. Different Plot Types

Plotly supports a wide array of plot types, allowing you to visualize data in various ways.

Bar Charts

Bar charts are useful for comparing quantities across different categories.

python

code

```python
# Create a bar chart
df_bar = pd.DataFrame({
    "Category": ["A", "B", "C"],
    "Values": [4, 7, 1]
})

fig = px.bar(df_bar, x="Category", y="Values", title="Bar Chart Example")
fig.show()
```

Line Charts

Line charts are excellent for showing trends over time.

python

code

```python
# Create a line chart
```

```python
df_line = pd.DataFrame({
    "Time": ["Jan", "Feb", "Mar", "Apr"],
    "Value": [10, 15, 13, 17]
})

fig = px.line(df_line, x="Time", y="Value", title="Line Chart Example")
fig.show()
```

Heatmaps

Heatmaps are effective for visualizing matrix-like data.

python

 code

```python
# Create a heatmap
import numpy as np

data = np.random.rand(10, 10)
fig = px.imshow(data, title="Heatmap Example")
fig.show()
```

5. Subplots

You can create complex layouts with multiple plots using the make_subplots function.

python

 code

```python
from plotly.subplots import make_subplots

# Create a 2x1 subplot
fig = make_subplots(rows=2, cols=1)

# Add a scatter plot to the first subplot
fig.add_trace(px.scatter(df, x="x", y="y").data[0], row=1, col=1)

# Add a bar plot to the second subplot
```

```python
fig.add_trace(px.bar(df_bar, x="Category", y="Values").data[0], row=2, col=1)

fig.update_layout(title_text="Subplot Example")
fig.show()
```

6. Dashboards with Plotly Dash

Plotly Dash enables users to create interactive web applications and dashboards. You can combine multiple visualizations into a single dashboard for comprehensive data analysis.

python

code

```python
# Sample Dash app (requires Dash installation)
from dash import Dash, dcc, html

app = Dash(__name__)

app.layout = html.Div([
    dcc.Graph(figure=fig),  # Use the figure created earlier
])

if __name__ == '__main__':
    app.run_server(debug=True)
```

Real-World Applications of Plotly

1. Data Analysis

Plotly is widely used for exploratory data analysis (EDA), allowing data scientists to visualize data distributions, relationships, and trends interactively.

2. Business Intelligence

Businesses leverage Plotly to create dashboards that visualize key performance indicators (KPIs), sales data, and customer insights, facilitating informed decision-making.

3. Scientific Research

Researchers use Plotly for data visualization in scientific studies, presenting complex datasets and findings in an understandable manner.

4. Web Applications

With Plotly Dash, developers can build interactive web applications that allow users to explore data and generate insights on the fly.

5. Education

Plotly is used in educational settings to teach data visualization concepts, helping students understand data analysis through interactive examples.

Conclusion

Plotly is a powerful library for creating interactive visualizations and dashboards in Python. Its ability to produce engaging and informative plots makes it an essential tool for data scientists, analysts, and developers. With its extensive support for various plot types, customization options, and integration with web applications, Plotly enables users to explore and communicate data insights effectively.

By mastering Plotly, you can enhance your data visualization capabilities, create compelling dashboards, and present data-driven insights that drive decision-making and foster collaboration. Whether you are analyzing datasets, presenting findings, or building interactive applications, Plotly provides the tools necessary to bring your data to life.

NLTK: A Comprehensive Overview for Natural Language Processing

Introduction to NLTK

The Natural Language Toolkit (NLTK) is a powerful library in Python designed for working with human language data (text). It provides a suite of tools and resources for processing natural language, making it an invaluable resource for researchers, educators, and developers in the field of Natural Language Processing (NLP). Developed by Steven Bird and Edward Loper, NLTK offers easy access to a wide range of lexical resources, including corpora, linguistic data, and tools for text processing and analysis.

Key Features of NLTK

1. **Extensive Text Processing Capabilities**: NLTK supports tokenization, stemming, lemmatization, parsing, and more, allowing for comprehensive text analysis.

2. **Access to Linguistic Resources**: The library includes a vast collection of corpora and lexical resources, such as WordNet, providing users with rich linguistic data.

3. **Built-in Classifiers**: NLTK includes various classification algorithms and tools for building machine learning models for text classification tasks.
4. **Visualization Tools**: NLTK offers visualization capabilities to help users better understand their data and analysis results.
5. **Educational Focus**: NLTK is designed with education in mind, making it accessible for beginners while also providing depth for advanced users.

Core Components of NLTK

1. Installation

To get started with NLTK, you need to install it via pip and download the necessary data packages.

bash

 code

```
pip install nltk
```

Then, in a Python script or interpreter, download the datasets:

python

 code

```
import nltk
nltk.download('popular')  # Downloads popular datasets and models
```

2. Text Processing

Tokenization

Tokenization is the process of splitting text into individual words or sentences.

python

 code

```
from nltk.tokenize import word_tokenize, sent_tokenize

text = "Natural Language Processing is fascinating. Let's explore NLTK!"

# Tokenize into words
words = word_tokenize(text)
print(words)

# Tokenize into sentences
```

```python
sentences = sent_tokenize(text)
print(sentences)
```

Stemming and Lemmatization

Stemming reduces words to their root form, while lemmatization converts words to their base form based on their meanings.

python

code

```python
from nltk.stem import PorterStemmer
from nltk.stem import WordNetLemmatizer

# Stemming
stemmer = PorterStemmer()
print([stemmer.stem(word) for word in words])

# Lemmatization
lemmatizer = WordNetLemmatizer()
print([lemmatizer.lemmatize(word) for word in words])
```

3. Part-of-Speech Tagging

NLTK can assign parts of speech to words, helping to understand their grammatical roles in sentences.

python

code

```python
from nltk import pos_tag

# Part-of-speech tagging
tagged_words = pos_tag(words)
print(tagged_words)
```

4. Named Entity Recognition (NER)

Named Entity Recognition identifies and classifies named entities in text, such as people, organizations, and locations.

python

code

from nltk import ne_chunk

Named entity recognition

named_entities = ne_chunk(tagged_words)

print(named_entities)

5. Working with Corpora

NLTK provides access to a variety of corpora, which are large collections of texts used for linguistic research.

python

code

from nltk.corpus import gutenberg

Load a text from the Gutenberg corpus

gutenberg_text = gutenberg.raw('austen-emma.txt')

print(gutenberg_text[:500]) # Print the first 500 characters

6. Classification

NLTK includes built-in classifiers for text classification tasks, such as sentiment analysis.

python

code

from nltk.classify import NaiveBayesClassifier

Sample training data

train_data = [('I love this movie', 'pos'), ('This film is terrible', 'neg')]

train_data = [(nltk.word_tokenize(text), label) for (text, label) in train_data]

Feature extraction

def extract_features(words):

    return {word: True for word in words}

Create a feature set

```python
featuresets = [(extract_features(words), label) for (words, label) in train_data]

# Train the classifier
classifier = NaiveBayesClassifier.train(featuresets)

# Test the classifier
test_text = "What a great movie!"
test_features = extract_features(nltk.word_tokenize(test_text))
print(classifier.classify(test_features))  # Output: 'pos'
```

7. Visualization

NLTK also provides tools for visualizing the results of text processing and analysis.

python

code

```python
import matplotlib.pyplot as plt
from nltk import FreqDist

# Frequency distribution of words
fdist = FreqDist(words)
fdist.plot(30, cumulative=False)
plt.title("Word Frequency Distribution")
plt.show()
```

Real-World Applications of NLTK

1. Text Classification

NLTK is widely used for tasks such as spam detection, sentiment analysis, and topic classification, enabling automated categorization of text.

2. Information Extraction

Organizations use NLTK for extracting meaningful information from unstructured data, such as resumes, articles, and customer feedback.

3. Chatbots and Virtual Assistants

NLTK helps in developing natural language understanding components for chatbots and virtual assistants, enhancing user interactions.

4. Linguistic Research

Researchers use NLTK for computational linguistics and linguistic analysis, allowing for the exploration of language patterns and structures.

5. Educational Tools

NLTK is often employed in academia to teach concepts in NLP and computational linguistics, providing practical examples and hands-on experience.

Conclusion

The Natural Language Toolkit (NLTK) is an essential library for anyone working with natural language data in Python. With its extensive text processing capabilities, access to linguistic resources, and built-in classifiers, NLTK empowers users to conduct sophisticated text analysis and build NLP applications. Its educational focus makes it particularly accessible for beginners, while its depth caters to advanced users.

By mastering NLTK, you can enhance your skills in text processing and analysis, develop applications for various NLP tasks, and contribute to the evolving field of natural language processing. Whether you are working on sentiment analysis, chatbots, or linguistic research, NLTK provides the tools necessary to unlock the potential of human language data.

SpaCy:

A Comprehensive Overview for Efficient Natural Language Processing

Introduction to SpaCy

SpaCy is an open-source library for advanced Natural Language Processing (NLP) in Python, designed specifically for production use. It emphasizes performance and efficiency, making it a popular choice among data scientists and developers for a wide range of NLP tasks. With its focus on ease of use, SpaCy provides pre-trained models that enable quick and accurate analysis of text data, making it suitable for both academic research and real-world applications.

Key Features of SpaCy

1. **Fast and Efficient**: Built for performance, SpaCy is optimized for speed, allowing for quick processing of large volumes of text.

2. **Pre-trained Models**: SpaCy offers a variety of pre-trained models for multiple languages, covering various tasks like part-of-speech tagging, named entity recognition, and dependency parsing.

3. **Robust API**: The library provides a clean and intuitive API that simplifies complex NLP tasks, making it easy to integrate into applications.

4. **Pipeline Architecture**: SpaCy uses a customizable processing pipeline, allowing users to tailor the flow of text processing according to their needs.

5. **Deep Learning Integration**: SpaCy can be seamlessly integrated with deep learning libraries like TensorFlow and PyTorch, enhancing its capabilities for advanced NLP tasks.

Core Components of SpaCy

1. Installation

To get started with SpaCy, install the library and download a pre-trained language model.

bash

code

pip install spacy

python -m spacy download en_core_web_sm # Download the small English model

2. Basic Usage

To begin processing text, you need to load the language model and create a Doc object.

python

 code

import spacy

\# Load the English model

nlp = spacy.load("en_core_web_sm")

\# Process text

text = "SpaCy is an efficient library for natural language processing."

doc = nlp(text)

\# Accessing tokens

for token in doc:

   print(token.text, token.lemma_, token.pos_, token.dep_)

3. Tokenization

Tokenization in SpaCy is efficient and easy, allowing you to split text into individual tokens seamlessly.

python

 code

tokens = [token.text for token in doc]

print(tokens)

4. Part-of-Speech Tagging

SpaCy automatically assigns part-of-speech tags to each token, helping to understand their grammatical roles.

python

 code

```
for token in doc:
    print(token.text, token.pos_)
```

5. Named Entity Recognition (NER)

SpaCy excels in named entity recognition, identifying entities like people, organizations, and locations within text.

python

 code

```
for ent in doc.ents:
    print(ent.text, ent.label_)
```

6. Dependency Parsing

Dependency parsing helps understand the grammatical structure of sentences by identifying relationships between words.

python

 code

```
for token in doc:
    print(f"{token.text} --> {token.head.text} ({token.dep_})")
```

7. Sentence Segmentation

SpaCy can also segment text into individual sentences, making it easy to analyze larger texts.

python

 code

```
for sentence in doc.sents:
    print(sentence.text)
```

8. Custom Pipeline Components

SpaCy allows users to add custom processing components to the NLP pipeline, providing flexibility for specific tasks.

python

 code

```
def custom_component(doc):
    # Example: Print the length of the document
    print(f"Document length: {len(doc)}")
    return doc
```

```python
# Add custom component to the pipeline
nlp.add_pipe(custom_component, last=True)
doc = nlp("SpaCy is great for NLP.")
```

9. Visualizing Results

SpaCy provides tools for visualizing the syntactic structure of sentences, which can be helpful for analysis.

python

 code

```
from spacy import displacy

# Visualize dependency parse
displacy.render(doc, style="dep", jupyter=True)
```

10. Integration with Deep Learning

SpaCy can be integrated with popular deep learning libraries to enhance its NLP capabilities, allowing for custom model training.

python

 code

```
import spacy
from spacy.training import Example

# Example of integrating with a deep learning model
# Load model, prepare data, and create training examples...
```

Real-World Applications of SpaCy

1. Information Extraction

SpaCy is used for extracting valuable information from unstructured text, such as resumes, articles, and customer feedback.

2. Chatbots and Virtual Assistants

Developers utilize SpaCy for building natural language understanding components in chatbots and virtual assistants, improving user interaction.

3. Sentiment Analysis

With its robust capabilities, SpaCy can be used to analyze sentiment in text data, helping organizations understand customer feedback and opinions.

4. Text Classification

SpaCy can facilitate text classification tasks, allowing users to categorize large volumes of text based on content or themes.

5. Academic Research

Researchers leverage SpaCy for linguistic studies and experiments, thanks to its efficiency and extensive capabilities.

Conclusion

SpaCy is a powerful and efficient library for Natural Language Processing that provides users with the tools necessary for processing and analyzing human language data. Its focus on performance, ease of use, and robust functionality makes it suitable for a wide range of applications, from academic research to real-world software development.

By mastering SpaCy, you can enhance your NLP skills, build sophisticated language models, and develop applications that leverage the power of human language data. Whether you are performing sentiment analysis, building chatbots, or conducting linguistic research, SpaCy offers the features and efficiency needed to succeed in the dynamic field of NLP.

Transformers (Hugging Face): A Comprehensive Overview for State-of-the-Art NLP

Introduction to Hugging Face Transformers

Hugging Face Transformers is an open-source library designed for Natural Language Processing (NLP) that provides access to a wide range of state-of-the-art pre-trained models. This library makes it easier for researchers and developers to utilize advanced models like BERT, GPT, T5, and many others for various NLP tasks, including text classification, translation, summarization, and more. With a focus on ease of use and community-driven development, Hugging Face has become a leader in the field of NLP.

Key Features of Hugging Face Transformers

1. **Wide Range of Pre-trained Models**: Offers numerous pre-trained models for various tasks and languages, allowing users to leverage powerful architectures without extensive training.

2. **Easy Fine-tuning**: Provides simple APIs for fine-tuning models on custom datasets, enabling users to adapt models for specific applications.

3. **Tokenization and Input Processing**: Includes robust tokenization tools that prepare input data for models, ensuring compatibility and optimal performance.

4. **Integration with Popular Frameworks**: Compatible with TensorFlow and PyTorch, allowing flexibility depending on user preference.

5. **Community and Ecosystem**: A vibrant community contributes to the library, creating an ecosystem of resources, tutorials, and shared models.

Core Components of Hugging Face Transformers

1. Installation

To get started with Hugging Face Transformers, install the library via pip:

bash

 code

```
pip install transformers
```

2. Basic Usage

You can quickly load a pre-trained model and tokenizer for a specific task.

python

 code

```
from transformers import pipeline

# Load a pre-trained model for sentiment analysis
classifier = pipeline('sentiment-analysis')

# Make predictions
result = classifier("I love using Hugging Face Transformers!")
print(result)
```

3. Tokenization

Tokenization is a crucial step in NLP, and Hugging Face provides simple tools for converting text into the appropriate input format for models.

python

 code

```
from transformers import AutoTokenizer

# Load a tokenizer
tokenizer = AutoTokenizer.from_pretrained("bert-base-uncased")

# Tokenize input text
```

```python
text = "Hello, how are you?"
tokens = tokenizer(text, return_tensors='pt')
print(tokens)
```

4. Fine-Tuning Models

Hugging Face makes it easy to fine-tune pre-trained models on custom datasets. Below is a simplified example of how to fine-tune a model for text classification.

python

 code

```python
from transformers import AutoModelForSequenceClassification, Trainer, TrainingArguments
from datasets import load_dataset

# Load dataset
dataset = load_dataset("imdb")

# Load pre-trained model
model = AutoModelForSequenceClassification.from_pretrained("distilbert-base-uncased", num_labels=2)

# Define training arguments
training_args = TrainingArguments(
    output_dir='./results',
    num_train_epochs=3,
    per_device_train_batch_size=16,
    evaluation_strategy="epoch",
)

# Create Trainer instance
trainer = Trainer(
    model=model,
    args=training_args,
    train_dataset=dataset['train'],
```

```
    eval_dataset=dataset['test']
)
```

Start training

trainer.train()

5. Model Inference

Once fine-tuning is complete, you can use the model to make predictions on new data.

python

 code

Use the fine-tuned model for inference

input_text = "This movie was fantastic!"

input_tokens = tokenizer(input_text, return_tensors='pt')

predictions = model(**input_tokens)

6. Using Transformers for Various NLP Tasks

Hugging Face Transformers supports a wide array of NLP tasks. Here are a few examples:

Text Generation

Using models like GPT-2 for text generation is straightforward.

python

 code

generator = pipeline('text-generation', model='gpt2')

output = generator("Once upon a time", max_length=50)

print(output)

Named Entity Recognition (NER)

You can easily perform NER with a pre-trained model.

python

 code

ner_model = pipeline('ner', aggregation_strategy="simple")

entities = ner_model("Hugging Face is based in New York City.")

print(entities)

Question Answering

For tasks like question answering, Hugging Face provides dedicated pipelines.

python

 code

```python
qa_pipeline = pipeline('question-answering')

result = qa_pipeline(question="What is Hugging Face?", context="Hugging Face is an AI company.")

print(result)
```

7. Model Sharing and Community

Hugging Face provides a model hub where users can share their models with the community. You can load models directly from the hub.

python

 code

```python
# Load a model shared by the community
community_model = AutoModelForSequenceClassification.from_pretrained("your-username/your-model")
```

8. Visualizing Model Performance

Using libraries like Matplotlib or Seaborn, you can visualize the performance of models based on metrics like accuracy, loss, and more.

python

 code

```python
import matplotlib.pyplot as plt


# Example visualization (custom data)
plt.plot(range(epochs), training_losses, label='Training Loss')

plt.xlabel('Epochs')

plt.ylabel('Loss')

plt.title('Training Loss Over Epochs')

plt.legend()

plt.show()
```

Real-World Applications of Hugging Face Transformers

1. Text Classification

Hugging Face Transformers are widely used for tasks like sentiment analysis, topic classification, and spam detection.

2. Machine Translation

The library supports models for translating text between multiple languages, making it useful for global applications.

3. Content Generation

Developers use Hugging Face for generating creative content, such as writing assistance, story generation, and dialogue systems.

4. Question Answering Systems

Businesses leverage these models for building chatbots and customer support systems that can answer user queries effectively.

5. Research and Development

Hugging Face is popular in academia for conducting research in NLP, enabling rapid prototyping and experimentation with state-of-the-art models.

Conclusion

Hugging Face Transformers has revolutionized the way practitioners and researchers approach Natural Language Processing by providing easy access to state-of-the-art models and a user-friendly interface for fine-tuning and deployment. Its rich ecosystem, robust community support, and integration with deep learning frameworks make it an essential tool for anyone working in NLP.

By mastering Hugging Face Transformers, you can leverage the latest advancements in NLP to build powerful applications, perform sophisticated analyses, and contribute to the ever-evolving field of natural language understanding. Whether you're working on sentiment analysis, translation, or content generation, Hugging Face provides the resources and tools necessary to succeed.

OpenCV: A Comprehensive Overview for Computer Vision Tasks

Introduction to OpenCV

OpenCV (Open Source Computer Vision Library) is an open-source computer vision and machine learning software library that provides a comprehensive set of tools for processing images and videos. Originally developed by Intel, it is now maintained by Willow Garage and later Itseez (which was later renamed OpenCV.org). With over 2500 optimized algorithms, OpenCV supports a wide range of computer vision tasks, making it one of the most popular libraries in the field.

Key Features of OpenCV

1. **Extensive Functionality**: OpenCV provides algorithms for image processing, object detection, face recognition, motion analysis, and much more.
2. **Cross-Platform**: It runs on various platforms, including Windows, Linux, macOS, Android, and iOS, making it versatile for application development.
3. **Integration with Other Libraries**: OpenCV can be easily integrated with other libraries, such as NumPy for numerical operations, TensorFlow, and PyTorch for deep learning applications.
4. **Real-Time Processing**: Designed for real-time computer vision, OpenCV is optimized for performance, enabling quick processing of images and video streams.
5. **Active Community**: A large community of developers and researchers contributes to OpenCV, providing tutorials, documentation, and updates.

Core Components of OpenCV

1. Installation

To get started with OpenCV, install it using pip:

bash

```
pip install opencv-python
```

You may also want to install additional packages for GUI support and image I/O:

bash

```
pip install opencv-python-headless  # For server environments without GUI
pip install opencv-contrib-python    # For extra modules
```

2. Basic Usage

You can load, display, and manipulate images using OpenCV easily.

python

```
import cv2

# Load an image
image = cv2.imread('image.jpg')
```

```python
# Display the image in a window
cv2.imshow('Image', image)
cv2.waitKey(0)  # Wait for a key press
cv2.destroyAllWindows()
```

3. Image Processing

OpenCV provides a variety of image processing functions, such as resizing, blurring, and color space conversion.

Resizing an Image

python

 code

```python
# Resize the image
resized_image = cv2.resize(image, (300, 300))
```

Converting Color Spaces

python

 code

```python
# Convert to grayscale
gray_image = cv2.cvtColor(image, cv2.COLOR_BGR2GRAY)
```

Blurring an Image

python

 code

```python
# Apply Gaussian blur
blurred_image = cv2.GaussianBlur(image, (5, 5), 0)
```

4. Image Thresholding

Thresholding is a technique used to segment images. OpenCV provides several thresholding methods.

python

 code

```python
# Convert to grayscale
gray = cv2.cvtColor(image, cv2.COLOR_BGR2GRAY)
```

Apply binary thresholding

```python
_, thresh = cv2.threshold(gray, 127, 255, cv2.THRESH_BINARY)
```

5. Edge Detection

OpenCV includes algorithms for edge detection, such as the Canny edge detector.

python

 code

```python
# Canny edge detection
edges = cv2.Canny(image, 100, 200)
```

6. Contour Detection

Contours are useful for shape analysis and object detection.

python

 code

```python
# Find contours
contours, _ = cv2.findContours(thresh, cv2.RETR_EXTERNAL, cv2.CHAIN_APPROX_SIMPLE)

# Draw contours on the image
cv2.drawContours(image, contours, -1, (0, 255, 0), 3)
```

7. Object Detection and Recognition

OpenCV supports various object detection techniques, including Haar cascades for face detection.

python

 code

```python
# Load the Haar cascade classifier for face detection
face_cascade = cv2.CascadeClassifier(cv2.data.haarcascades + 'haarcascade_frontalface_default.xml')

# Detect faces in the image
faces = face_cascade.detectMultiScale(gray, scaleFactor=1.1, minNeighbors=5)

# Draw rectangles around detected faces
```

```python
for (x, y, w, h) in faces:
    cv2.rectangle(image, (x, y), (x + w, y + h), (255, 0, 0), 2)
```

8. Video Processing

OpenCV can also process video files or streams from a camera.

python
 code

```python
# Capture video from the webcam
cap = cv2.VideoCapture(0)

while True:
    ret, frame = cap.read()
    if not ret:
        break

    # Process the frame (e.g., convert to grayscale)
    gray_frame = cv2.cvtColor(frame, cv2.COLOR_BGR2GRAY)

    # Display the processed frame
    cv2.imshow('Video', gray_frame)

    if cv2.waitKey(1) & 0xFF == ord('q'):
        break

cap.release()
cv2.destroyAllWindows()
```

9. Feature Detection and Matching

OpenCV includes algorithms for feature detection, such as SIFT, SURF, and ORB.

python
 code

```python
# Initialize ORB detector
```

```
orb = cv2.ORB_create()
```

Find keypoints and descriptors

```
keypoints, descriptors = orb.detectAndCompute(gray_image, None)
```

Draw keypoints on the image

```
image_with_keypoints = cv2.drawKeypoints(image, keypoints, None, color=(0, 255, 0))
```

10. Machine Learning Integration

OpenCV provides support for integrating machine learning models for tasks such as object detection and classification.

python

code

```
from sklearn import datasets
from sklearn.model_selection import train_test_split
from sklearn.svm import SVC
```

Example of using an SVM model with OpenCV for classification

Load dataset, preprocess, train and evaluate the model...

Real-World Applications of OpenCV

1. Facial Recognition

OpenCV is widely used in security systems for facial recognition applications.

2. Object Tracking

Applications like surveillance, sports analytics, and robotics utilize OpenCV for tracking objects in video feeds.

3. Medical Image Processing

In healthcare, OpenCV is used for analyzing medical images, such as MRI scans and X-rays.

4. Augmented Reality

OpenCV enables developers to build augmented reality applications by integrating virtual objects into real-world environments.

5. Autonomous Vehicles

OpenCV plays a crucial role in computer vision for autonomous vehicles, aiding in object detection, lane detection, and obstacle avoidance.

Conclusion

OpenCV is a powerful and versatile library for computer vision that provides a rich set of tools for image and video processing. Its wide range of algorithms, cross-platform support, and integration capabilities make it a popular choice for developers and researchers working in computer vision.

By mastering OpenCV, you can tackle various computer vision tasks, from basic image processing to complex machine learning applications. Whether you're developing applications in security, healthcare, robotics, or augmented reality, OpenCV offers the tools necessary to bring your ideas to life.

FastAI: A Comprehensive Overview for Simplified Neural Network Training

Introduction to FastAI

FastAI is an open-source deep learning library built on top of PyTorch, designed to simplify the process of training neural networks for various tasks, including image classification, natural language processing, and tabular data. Its primary goal is to make deep learning accessible to practitioners and researchers by providing high-level abstractions and a user-friendly interface, while still maintaining the flexibility and power of the underlying PyTorch framework.

Key Features of FastAI

1. **High-Level API**: FastAI offers a high-level interface that abstracts away much of the boilerplate code required for training deep learning models, making it easier to experiment and iterate.

2. **Pre-trained Models**: The library provides a wide range of pre-trained models, allowing users to leverage transfer learning for their tasks, thus speeding up the training process and improving performance.

3. **Data Handling**: FastAI includes powerful data loading and transformation utilities, making it easy to preprocess and augment datasets.
4. **Built-in Callbacks**: The library features a callback system that allows users to customize training behavior, implement early stopping, logging, and model checkpointing.
5. **Community and Documentation**: FastAI has a strong community and extensive documentation, including tutorials and courses that help users learn deep learning concepts and practical applications.

Core Components of FastAI

1. Installation

To get started with FastAI, you can install it using pip. Ensure that you have the required dependencies:

bash

```
code
```

pip install fastai

2. Basic Usage

FastAI provides a straightforward way to create and train models. Here's a simple example of how to train an image classification model.

python

```
code
```

from fastai.vision.all import *

# Load a dataset (e.g., CIFAR-10)
path = untar_data(URLs.CIFAR)

# Create a DataBlock
data = DataBlock(blocks=(ImageBlock, CategoryBlock),
        getters=[ColReader('fname'), ColReader('label')],
        splitter=RandomSplitter(valid_pct=0.2),
        item_tfms=Resize(224))

# Create a DataLoaders object
dls = data.dataloaders(path/'train.csv')

```python
# Create a CNN learner
learn = cnn_learner(dls, resnet34, metrics=accuracy)

# Train the model
learn.fine_tune(1)
```

3. Data Handling

FastAI simplifies data handling through its DataBlock API, which allows for flexible data loading and augmentation.

Data Augmentation

Data augmentation can significantly improve model performance by artificially increasing the diversity of the training dataset.

python

code

```python
data = DataBlock(blocks=(ImageBlock, CategoryBlock),
                 get_items=get_image_files,
                 splitter=RandomSplitter(),
                 item_tfms=Resize(224),
                 batch_tfms=aug_transforms())
```

4. Transfer Learning

FastAI makes it easy to utilize transfer learning with pre-trained models.

python

code

```python
learn = cnn_learner(dls, resnet50, metrics=accuracy)
learn.fine_tune(3)
```

5. Callbacks

Callbacks in FastAI allow you to customize training behavior. You can use built-in callbacks or create your own.

python

code

```python
# Using a built-in callback for early stopping
```

learn.fit_one_cycle(5, callbacks=[EarlyStoppingCallback(learn, patience=2)])

6. Hyperparameter Tuning

FastAI provides tools for hyperparameter tuning, making it easy to find optimal settings for your model.

python

 code

learn.lr_find() # Find the optimal learning rate

learn.recorder.plot_lr_find()

7. Model Interpretation

FastAI includes tools for interpreting models, helping you understand how your model makes predictions.

python

 code

Show a confusion matrix

learn.show_confusion_matrix()

8. Exporting and Deployment

Once you've trained a model, you can easily export it for deployment.

python

 code

learn.export('my_model.pkl')

9. Multi-task Learning

FastAI supports multi-task learning, allowing you to train models for multiple related tasks simultaneously.

python

 code

Define a multi-task model

learn = cnn_learner(dls, resnet34, metrics=[accuracy, F1Score()])

learn.fit_one_cycle(5)

10. Integration with Other Libraries

FastAI integrates well with other libraries, such as Hugging Face Transformers for NLP tasks or OpenCV for image processing.

python

code

from fastai.text.all import *

Load text data for NLP tasks

data = TextDataLoaders.from_df(df, text_col='text', label_col='label')

learn = text_classifier_learner(data, pretrained_model='bert-base-uncased')

learn.fine_tune(3)

Real-World Applications of FastAI

1. Image Classification

FastAI is extensively used for building image classification models across various domains, from medical imaging to wildlife identification.

2. Natural Language Processing

With its support for NLP tasks, FastAI enables users to build models for sentiment analysis, text classification, and language translation.

3. Tabular Data Analysis

FastAI can also be applied to tabular data, making it suitable for tasks like regression and classification in structured datasets.

4. Transfer Learning for Custom Datasets

Users can leverage pre-trained models on custom datasets to achieve high accuracy with limited data.

5. Educational Purposes

FastAI is popular in academia and industry for teaching deep learning concepts, thanks to its accessible interface and extensive documentation.

Conclusion

FastAI is a powerful library that simplifies the process of building and training neural networks for various tasks. By providing a high-level API built on PyTorch, it enables users to focus on experimentation and model development rather than boilerplate code.

With features like easy data handling, transfer learning, and extensive community resources, FastAI empowers practitioners and researchers to tackle complex deep learning problems efficiently. Whether you're working on image classification, natural language processing, or tabular data, FastAI provides the tools you need to succeed in your deep learning projects.

Docker: A Comprehensive Overview for Model

Deployment and Serving

Introduction to Docker

Docker is an open-source platform that enables developers to automate the deployment of applications inside lightweight, portable containers. Containers package an application along with its dependencies, configurations, and libraries, ensuring that it runs consistently across different environments. This is particularly beneficial for deploying machine learning models, as it simplifies the process of moving models from development to production.

Key Features of Docker

1. **Portability**: Docker containers can run on any system that supports Docker, making it easy to deploy applications across different environments (development, testing, production).
2. **Isolation**: Each container operates in its own environment, preventing conflicts between applications and ensuring that they run independently of one another.
3. **Scalability**: Docker supports orchestration tools like Kubernetes, allowing for easy scaling of applications to handle varying workloads.
4. **Version Control**: Docker images can be versioned, enabling easy rollback to previous versions of applications if needed.
5. **Ecosystem**: The Docker ecosystem includes Docker Hub, a repository for sharing container images, and a wide range of tools for building, managing, and deploying containers.

Core Components of Docker

1. Installation

To get started with Docker, install Docker Desktop, which provides a complete development environment for building and managing containers.

- For Windows and macOS, download from the Docker website.
- For Linux, follow the installation instructions for your specific distribution.

2. Basic Concepts

Images and Containers

- **Images**: A Docker image is a read-only template that contains the application and its dependencies.

- **Containers**: A container is a runnable instance of an image. It includes everything needed to run the application.

Dockerfile

A Dockerfile is a text file that contains instructions for building a Docker image.

dockerfile

 code

```
# Example Dockerfile for a Flask app
FROM python:3.8-slim

# Set the working directory
WORKDIR /app

# Copy the requirements file and install dependencies
COPY requirements.txt .
RUN pip install -r requirements.txt

# Copy the application code
COPY . .

# Expose the application port
EXPOSE 5000

# Command to run the application
CMD ["python", "app.py"]
```

3. Building a Docker Image

You can build a Docker image from a Dockerfile using the following command:

bash

 code

```
docker build -t my-flask-app .
```

4. Running a Docker Container

Once the image is built, you can run a container from it:

bash

 code

docker run -p 5000:5000 my-flask-app

This command maps port 5000 on your host machine to port 5000 on the container, allowing you to access the application.

5. Managing Containers

You can list running containers, stop, and remove them using Docker commands:

bash

 code

List running containers

docker ps

Stop a container

docker stop <container_id>

Remove a container

docker rm <container_id>

6. Docker Compose

Docker Compose is a tool for defining and running multi-container Docker applications using a docker-compose.yml file. This is especially useful for applications that require multiple services, such as a web server and a database.

yaml

 code

version: '3'

services:
  web:
    build: .
    ports:
      - "5000:5000"
  db:

```
    image: postgres
    environment:
      POSTGRES_DB: mydb
      POSTGRES_USER: user
      POSTGRES_PASSWORD: password
```

Run the application with:

bash

 code

docker-compose up

7. Model Deployment

To deploy a machine learning model with Docker, you typically follow these steps:

1. **Create a Flask or FastAPI Application**: Wrap your model inference code in a web application to serve predictions.
2. **Define a Dockerfile**: Include all dependencies and configurations in a Dockerfile.
3. **Build the Image**: Use the docker build command.
4. **Run the Container**: Use the docker run command to deploy the application.

8. Serving Models with Flask

Here's a simple example of serving a machine learning model using Flask and Docker.

python

 code

```python
# app.py
from flask import Flask, request, jsonify
import joblib

app = Flask(__name__)
model = joblib.load('model.pkl')

@app.route('/predict', methods=['POST'])
def predict():
    data = request.json
    prediction = model.predict([data['features']])
```

```
    return jsonify(prediction.tolist())

if __name__ == '__main__':
    app.run(host='0.0.0.0', port=5000)
```

9. Docker Hub

Docker Hub is a cloud-based repository for sharing Docker images. You can push your images to Docker Hub to make them accessible from anywhere.

bash

 code

```bash
# Log in to Docker Hub
docker login


# Tag the image
docker tag my-flask-app myusername/my-flask-app


# Push the image
docker push myusername/my-flask-app
```

10. Orchestration with Kubernetes

For production deployments, Docker can be integrated with Kubernetes to manage containers at scale. Kubernetes automates the deployment, scaling, and management of containerized applications.

Real-World Applications of Docker

1. Microservices Architecture

Docker is commonly used in microservices architectures, allowing teams to develop, test, and deploy services independently.

2. Continuous Integration/Continuous Deployment (CI/CD)

Docker is integral to CI/CD pipelines, enabling automated testing and deployment of applications in a consistent environment.

3. Data Science and Machine Learning

Data scientists use Docker to package their models and dependencies, ensuring that they run consistently across different environments, whether in development or production.

4. Development Environments

Docker allows developers to create isolated environments for different projects, preventing dependency conflicts and ensuring reproducibility.

5. Edge Computing

Docker enables the deployment of applications in edge computing environments, where lightweight containers can be deployed close to the data source.

Conclusion

Docker is a powerful tool for model deployment and serving, providing a consistent and efficient way to package applications and their dependencies. Its portability, isolation, and ease of use make it an essential part of modern software development, especially in the fields of data science and machine learning.

By mastering Docker, you can streamline your deployment workflows, ensure consistency across environments, and effectively manage applications in production. Whether you're deploying simple web applications or complex machine learning models, Docker provides the infrastructure you need to succeed.

Flask and FastAPI: Lightweight Web Frameworks for Building APIs to Serve Models

Introduction

Flask and FastAPI are two popular lightweight web frameworks in Python, designed for building APIs to serve machine learning models and other applications. Both frameworks have distinct features, advantages, and use cases, making them suitable for different scenarios in model deployment.

Flask: A Comprehensive Overview

Overview

Flask is a micro web framework that is simple to set up and use. It is well-suited for small to medium-sized applications, including APIs for serving machine learning models.

Key Features of Flask

1. **Simplicity**: Flask is easy to learn and use, making it ideal for beginners and quick development.

2. **Flexibility**: Flask is unopinionated, allowing developers to choose how they want to structure their applications.

3. **Extensible**: It supports extensions that add functionality, such as authentication and database integration.

4. **Large Community**: A rich ecosystem of libraries and a large community provide extensive resources and support.

Basic Usage

Here's a simple example of how to set up a Flask API to serve a machine learning model.

Installation

bash

 code

pip install Flask

Basic API Example

python

 code

```
from flask import Flask, request, jsonify
import joblib

app = Flask(__name__)
model = joblib.load('model.pkl')

@app.route('/predict', methods=['POST'])
def predict():
    data = request.json
    prediction = model.predict([data['features']])
    return jsonify(prediction.tolist())

if __name__ == '__main__':
    app.run(host='0.0.0.0', port=5000)
```

Running the Flask App

Run the application with:

bash

 code

python app.py

You can then send a POST request to http://localhost:5000/predict with JSON data to get predictions.

FastAPI: A Comprehensive Overview

Overview

FastAPI is a modern web framework for building APIs with Python. It is built on top of Starlette and Pydantic, offering high performance, automatic generation of OpenAPI documentation, and type checking.

Key Features of FastAPI

1. **Performance**: FastAPI is one of the fastest web frameworks available, thanks to its asynchronous capabilities.

2. **Type Annotations**: It leverages Python type hints to validate request data, making it easier to work with and debug.

3. **Automatic Documentation**: FastAPI automatically generates interactive API documentation (Swagger UI and ReDoc).

4. **Asynchronous Support**: Built-in support for asynchronous programming allows for handling multiple requests simultaneously.

Basic Usage

Here's how to set up a FastAPI application to serve a machine learning model.

Installation

bash

 code

pip install fastapi uvicorn

Basic API Example

python

 code

```
from fastapi import FastAPI

from pydantic import BaseModel

import joblib


app = FastAPI()

model = joblib.load('model.pkl')


class PredictionRequest(BaseModel):
    features: list


@app.post('/predict')
```

```python
def predict(request: PredictionRequest):
    prediction = model.predict([request.features])
    return {'prediction': prediction.tolist()}


if __name__ == '__main__':
    import uvicorn
    uvicorn.run(app, host='0.0.0.0', port=5000)
```

Running the FastAPI App

Run the application with:

bash

 code

```
uvicorn app:app --host 0.0.0.0 --port 5000 --reload
```

You can access the interactive documentation at http://localhost:5000/docs.

Comparing Flask and FastAPI

Feature	Flask	FastAPI
Speed	Moderate	High (async capabilities)
Type Checking	No	Yes (with Pydantic)
Automatic Documentation	No	Yes (Swagger UI and ReDoc)
Ease of Learning	Easy, great for beginners	Easy, but requires understanding of types
Use Case	Small to medium applications	High-performance APIs, real-time applications

When to Use Which Framework

- **Use Flask** when:
    - You need a simple, straightforward API.
    - You're building a small application or prototype.
    - You want more control over your application structure.
- **Use FastAPI** when:
    - Performance is a critical concern, and you want asynchronous capabilities.
    - You want automatic data validation and serialization with type hints.

- You need automatic API documentation for easier testing and exploration.

Conclusion

Flask and FastAPI are excellent choices for building APIs to serve machine learning models. Flask offers simplicity and flexibility, making it suitable for quick setups, while FastAPI provides high performance and automatic validation, ideal for larger applications. Depending on your project requirements, you can choose the framework that best fits your needs to deploy and serve your models effectively.

TensorFlow Serving: A Comprehensive Overview for Serving TensorFlow Models in Production

Introduction to TensorFlow Serving

TensorFlow Serving is an open-source library designed specifically for deploying machine learning models in production environments. It allows developers to manage and serve TensorFlow models efficiently, providing a flexible architecture to accommodate the complexities of production systems. With TensorFlow Serving, you can deploy models seamlessly, ensuring low-latency predictions and high throughput.

Key Features of TensorFlow Serving

1. **Model Management**: Supports versioning and management of multiple models, allowing for easy updates and rollbacks.
2. **High Performance**: Optimized for low-latency inference and can handle large volumes of requests, making it suitable for production environments.
3. **Extensible Architecture**: Can serve not only TensorFlow models but also models from other frameworks with custom plugins.
4. **RESTful API and gRPC Support**: Provides interfaces for easy integration with applications using REST or gRPC protocols.
5. **Monitoring and Logging**: Integrates with TensorFlow Model Analysis for monitoring model performance and logging requests and responses.

Core Components of TensorFlow Serving

1. Installation

You can install TensorFlow Serving using Docker, which is the recommended way due to its simplicity and isolation of dependencies.

bash

 code

```
# Pull the TensorFlow Serving Docker image
docker pull tensorflow/serving
```

2. Serving a Model

To serve a TensorFlow model, you first need to export your trained model using the TensorFlow SavedModel format.

Exporting a Model

python

 code

```
import tensorflow as tf


# Assuming you have a trained model
model = ... # Your trained model
```

```
# Save the model
tf.saved_model.save(model, 'path/to/saved_model')
```

Running TensorFlow Serving

You can serve the model using Docker with the following command:

bash

code

```
docker run -p 8501:8501 --name=tf_model_serving --mount type=bind,source=$(pwd)/path/to/saved_model,target=/models/my_model -e MODEL_NAME=my_model -t tensorflow/serving
```

This command does the following:

- Binds the local model directory to the container.
- Sets the model name to my_model.
- Exposes the model serving API on port 8501.

3. Making Predictions

You can make predictions by sending HTTP POST requests to the TensorFlow Serving API.

Example Prediction Request

bash

code

```
curl -d '{"signature_name":"serving_default", "instances":[{"input_1":[[1.0, 2.0, 3.0, 4.0]]}]}' -H "Content-Type: application/json" -X POST http://localhost:8501/v1/models/my_model:predict
```

4. gRPC Interface

TensorFlow Serving also supports gRPC for high-performance model serving. To use the gRPC interface, you need to install the TensorFlow library with gRPC support.

Example gRPC Client

You can use the TensorFlow Serving gRPC API to make predictions. Here's an example in Python:

python

code

```
import grpc
import tensorflow as tf
```

```python
from tensorflow_serving.apis import predict_pb2, prediction_service_pb2_grpc

channel = grpc.insecure_channel('localhost:8500')
stub = prediction_service_pb2_grpc.PredictionServiceStub(channel)

# Prepare the request
request = predict_pb2.PredictRequest()
request.model_spec.name = 'my_model'
request.model_spec.signature_name = 'serving_default'
request.inputs['input_1'].CopyFrom(tf.make_tensor_proto([[1.0, 2.0, 3.0, 4.0]]))

# Make the prediction
result = stub.Predict(request, timeout=10.0)
print(result)
```

5. Model Versioning

TensorFlow Serving supports model versioning, allowing you to deploy multiple versions of a model simultaneously. You can manage different versions by saving them in separate directories:

bash

 code

```
/models/my_model/1/
    saved_model.pb
/models/my_model/2/
    saved_model.pb
```

You can specify which version to serve using the --model_version_policy flag when starting TensorFlow Serving.

6. Monitoring and Logging

TensorFlow Serving integrates with TensorFlow Model Analysis (TMA) for monitoring your model's performance in production. It provides tools to visualize and analyze model predictions and drift over time.

7. Advanced Configurations

TensorFlow Serving allows for various configurations, such as:

- **Batching**: You can enable request batching to improve throughput.
- **Custom Metrics**: Implement custom metrics to monitor the serving performance and health.
- **Plugins**: Extend TensorFlow Serving to serve models from other frameworks by implementing custom loaders.

Real-World Applications of TensorFlow Serving

1. Productionizing Machine Learning Models

TensorFlow Serving is widely used in production environments to serve machine learning models, providing low-latency predictions for applications like recommendation systems, fraud detection, and more.

2. A/B Testing and Model Comparison

By supporting multiple model versions, TensorFlow Serving enables A/B testing and model comparison in production to evaluate the performance of different algorithms or model versions.

3. Real-Time Analytics

Applications that require real-time analytics benefit from TensorFlow Serving's ability to handle high-throughput requests efficiently, making it suitable for use cases in finance, healthcare, and e-commerce.

4. Multi-Model Serving

TensorFlow Serving allows for the deployment of multiple models in a single instance, which is beneficial for applications needing diverse predictions, such as image classification, natural language processing, and more.

Conclusion

TensorFlow Serving is an essential tool for deploying machine learning models in production, offering flexibility, performance, and ease of use. Its support for versioning, monitoring, and high-performance inference makes it an excellent choice for serving TensorFlow models.

By leveraging TensorFlow Serving, you can ensure that your models are available, scalable, and ready to provide predictions to your applications in real-time. Whether you're working on a small project or a large-scale application, TensorFlow Serving provides the infrastructure you need to succeed in model deployment.

MLflow: A Comprehensive Overview for Managing the

Machine Learning Lifecycle

Introduction to MLflow

MLflow is an open-source platform designed to manage the end-to-end machine learning lifecycle. It provides a suite of tools to help data scientists and machine learning engineers track experiments, reproduce results, and deploy models effectively. MLflow's modular architecture allows users to leverage its components independently or in combination, making it a versatile tool for managing machine learning projects.

Key Features of MLflow

1. **Experiment Tracking**: Record and compare parameters, metrics, and artifacts for multiple runs of experiments.

2. **Model Management**: Store and manage models from different frameworks in a central repository.

3. **Project Packaging**: Organize code into reproducible ML projects that can be shared and executed.

4. **Deployment**: Deploy models to various platforms, including cloud services and local environments, with ease.

5. **Integration**: Supports integration with popular libraries like TensorFlow, PyTorch, Scikit-learn, and more.

Core Components of MLflow

MLflow consists of four main components:

1. **MLflow Tracking**
2. **MLflow Projects**
3. **MLflow Models**
4. **MLflow Registry**

1. MLflow Tracking

MLflow Tracking is a component that allows you to log and query experiments. You can record metrics, parameters, and artifacts, making it easier to track the performance of different models.

Installation

To get started with MLflow, install it using pip:

bash

 code

pip install mlflow

Basic Usage

Here's a simple example of how to use MLflow for experiment tracking:

python

 code

```
import mlflow
import mlflow.sklearn
from sklearn.ensemble import RandomForestRegressor
from sklearn.datasets import load_boston
from sklearn.model_selection import train_test_split

# Load dataset
data = load_boston()
X_train, X_test, y_train, y_test = train_test_split(data.data, data.target, test_size=0.2, random_state=42)

# Start an MLflow run
with mlflow.start_run():
    # Train the model
    model = RandomForestRegressor()
    model.fit(X_train, y_train)

    # Log parameters
    mlflow.log_param("n_estimators", model.n_estimators)

    # Log metrics
    score = model.score(X_test, y_test)
    mlflow.log_metric("r2_score", score)
```

```python
# Log model
mlflow.sklearn.log_model(model, "model")
```

2. MLflow Projects

MLflow Projects allow you to organize your code into a structured format, making it easy to reproduce experiments. A project can be defined by a MLproject file that specifies dependencies and entry points.

Example of a Project Structure

code

```
my_project/
├── MLproject
├── conda.yaml
└── train.py
```

Example of MLproject File

yaml

```
code
name: My ML Project

conda_env: conda.yaml

entry_points:
  main:
    command: "python train.py"
```

Running a Project

You can run the project using the following command:

bash

```
code
mlflow run my_project
```

3. MLflow Models

MLflow Models provides a way to manage and serve machine learning models. It allows you to store models in a standard format, making it easy to deploy them across various platforms.

Logging a Model

You can log models from various frameworks (like Scikit-learn, TensorFlow, PyTorch) to MLflow:

python

 code

```
# Log a model
mlflow.sklearn.log_model(model, "my_model")
```

Serving a Model

MLflow makes it easy to serve models via a REST API:

bash

 code

```
mlflow models serve -m runs:/<run_id>/my_model -p 5000
```

You can then send HTTP requests to the API to make predictions.

4. MLflow Registry

The MLflow Model Registry is a centralized model store that allows you to manage models at different stages of their lifecycle (e.g., staging, production, archived). It provides a UI and APIs for versioning and managing model metadata.

Registering a Model

To register a model, you can use:

python

 code

```
mlflow.register_model("runs:/<run_id>/my_model", "MyModel")
```

Transitioning Models

You can transition models between stages using the registry:

python

 code

```
from mlflow.tracking import MlflowClient

client = MlflowClient()
client.transition_model_version_stage(
    name="MyModel",
    version=1,
```

```
    stage="Production"
)
```

Real-World Applications of MLflow

1. Experimentation and Hyperparameter Tuning

MLflow allows data scientists to track various hyperparameters and their impacts on model performance, facilitating better experimentation and fine-tuning.

2. Model Deployment

With its deployment capabilities, MLflow can be integrated into CI/CD pipelines, ensuring that the best-performing models are automatically promoted to production.

3. Collaboration

MLflow enables teams to share projects and models easily, fostering collaboration among data scientists and machine learning engineers.

4. Reproducibility

By tracking experiments and organizing code into projects, MLflow ensures that results can be reproduced, which is essential for both research and production environments.

Conclusion

MLflow is a powerful platform for managing the machine learning lifecycle, providing essential tools for tracking experiments, managing models, and facilitating deployment. Its modular architecture allows users to adopt the components that best fit their needs, making it an invaluable resource for data scientists and machine learning practitioners.

By incorporating MLflow into your workflow, you can enhance your productivity, ensure reproducibility, and streamline the deployment of machine learning models, ultimately leading to better and more efficient ML projects.

Weights & Biases: A Comprehensive Overview for Experiment Tracking and Collaboration

Introduction to Weights & Biases

Weights & Biases (WandB) is a powerful tool designed for experiment tracking, dataset versioning, and collaborative reporting in machine learning projects. It helps teams manage their workflows effectively by providing a unified platform to log experiments, visualize results, and collaborate seamlessly. WandB is particularly popular among data scientists and machine learning engineers for its ease of use and robust integration with popular machine learning libraries.

Key Features of Weights & Biases

1. **Experiment Tracking**: Log hyperparameters, metrics, and system performance in real-time to compare different experiments.

2. **Dataset Versioning**: Track changes in datasets and ensure reproducibility across experiments.
3. **Collaboration**: Share experiment results and visualizations with team members easily, fostering better communication and collaboration.
4. **Visualizations**: Create beautiful visualizations of metrics, comparisons, and more with -mal effort.
5. **Integrations**: Seamlessly integrates with popular libraries and frameworks like TensorFlow, PyTorch, Keras, Scikit-learn, and more.

Core Components of Weights & Biases

1. Installation

You can install Weights & Biases via pip:

bash

 code

pip install wandb

2. Setting Up a Project

To start using WandB, you need to initialize it in your script. This can be done by calling wandb.init().

Basic Usage

Here's a simple example demonstrating how to use WandB for experiment tracking:

python

 code

```
import wandb


# Initialize a new W&B run

wandb.init(project="my_ml_project")


# Log hyperparameters

config = wandb.config

config.epochs = 10

config.batch_size = 32


# Simulate training process
```

```
for epoch in range(config.epochs):

    # Simulate loss and accuracy values

    loss = 0.1 * (config.epochs - epoch)  # Dummy loss

    accuracy = (epoch + 1) / config.epochs  # Dummy accuracy


    # Log metrics

    wandb.log({"epoch": epoch, "loss": loss, "accuracy": accuracy})


# Finish the run

wandb.finish()
```

3. Experiment Tracking

WandB provides a dashboard to visualize logged metrics, compare different runs, and analyze model performance over time. You can track various parameters such as:

- Hyperparameters
- Loss and accuracy metrics
- System performance metrics (CPU/GPU usage, memory, etc.)

4. Visualizations

WandB allows you to create and customize visualizations for your logged metrics. The dashboard provides real-time updates and visual comparisons of experiments, making it easy to spot trends and issues.

5. Dataset Versioning

WandB also supports dataset versioning, allowing you to track and manage changes to your datasets effectively. This is especially useful in projects where datasets evolve over time.

Logging Datasets

You can log datasets to WandB by using:

python

 code

wandb.save("path/to/dataset")

6. Collaboration

WandB facilitates collaboration by enabling team members to view experiment results and visualizations in a shared dashboard. This feature enhances transparency and communication within teams, making it easier to discuss results and make informed decisions.

7. Integration with Popular Frameworks

WandB integrates seamlessly with popular machine learning frameworks, allowing you to log metrics and configurations without significant code changes. Here are some common integrations:

- **TensorFlow**: Automatically logs training metrics and visualizes them.
- **PyTorch**: Integrates with training loops for real-time logging.
- **Keras**: Provides callbacks to log metrics during model training.

Example Integration with PyTorch

Here's how to use WandB with a PyTorch training loop:

```python
code
import wandb
import torch

# Initialize W&B
wandb.init(project="my_pytorch_project")

# Define your model and optimizer
model = MyModel()
optimizer = torch.optim.Adam(model.parameters())

# Training loop
for epoch in range(epochs):
    for batch in dataloader:
        # Forward pass
        outputs = model(batch)
        loss = compute_loss(outputs, batch)

        # Backward pass
        optimizer.zero_grad()
        loss.backward()
```

```
        optimizer.step()

        # Log metrics
        wandb.log({"epoch": epoch, "loss": loss.item()})

# Finish the run
wandb.finish()
```

Real-World Applications of Weights & Biases

1. Experiment Management

WandB is widely used in research and production environments to manage experiments effectively, enabling teams to track multiple model iterations and hyperparameter configurations.

2. Model Evaluation

With its visualization capabilities, WandB helps teams evaluate model performance visually, making it easier to compare different models and configurations.

3. Collaborative Research

WandB's collaborative features enable teams to work together on projects, share findings, and communicate results in real time.

4. Reproducibility

By tracking datasets, hyperparameters, and metrics, WandB ensures that experiments are reproducible, which is essential for research and production environments.

Conclusion

Weights & Biases is a powerful tool for managing the machine learning workflow, offering essential features for experiment tracking, dataset versioning, and collaborative reporting. Its seamless integration with popular machine learning frameworks and user-friendly interface make it an invaluable resource for data scientists and machine learning engineers.

By incorporating Weights & Biases into your machine learning projects, you can enhance collaboration, ensure reproducibility, and streamline the process of tracking experiments and results, ultimately leading to more effective and efficient ML workflows.

Optuna: A Comprehensive Overview of Hyperparameter Optimization

Introduction to Optuna

Optuna is an open-source hyperparameter optimization framework designed to automate the tuning process in machine learning. It provides a flexible and efficient way to search for optimal hyperparameters, allowing data scientists and machine learning practitioners to improve model performance without extensive manual tuning. Optuna is particularly known for its ease of use, scalability, and support for modern optimization techniques.

Key Features of Optuna

1. **Automatic Search Algorithms**: Utilizes state-of-the-art algorithms such as Tree-structured Parzen Estimator (TPE) and Bayesian optimization.
2. **Pruning**: Automatically stops unpromising trials based on intermediate results, saving time and computational resources.
3. **Dynamic Search Space**: Allows for defining complex and dynamic search spaces, enabling more flexible hyperparameter tuning.
4. **Visualization Tools**: Provides built-in visualization tools for analyzing optimization results.
5. **Integration**: Easily integrates with popular machine learning libraries like TensorFlow, PyTorch, and Scikit-learn.

Core Components of Optuna

1. Installation

You can install Optuna using pip:

bash

 code

```
pip install optuna
```

2. Basic Usage

To get started with Optuna, you define an objective function that includes the hyperparameters you want to optimize. Here's a simple example using a hypothetical machine learning model:

Defining an Objective Function

python

 code

```
import optuna
import numpy as np

def objective(trial):
    # Suggest hyperparameters
    n_estimators = trial.suggest_int('n_estimators', 10, 100)
    max_depth = trial.suggest_int('max_depth', 1, 32)
```

```python
learning_rate = trial.suggest_float('learning_rate', 0.001, 0.1)

# Simulate model training and validation
model = MyModel(n_estimators=n_estimators, max_depth=max_depth, learning_rate=learning_rate)
model.fit(X_train, y_train)
accuracy = model.evaluate(X_val, y_val)

return accuracy
```

3. Running the Optimization

To perform the optimization, you create a study object and call the optimize method with the objective function and the number of trials:

python

 code

```python
study = optuna.create_study(direction='maximize')
study.optimize(objective, n_trials=100)
```

4. Accessing the Results

After the optimization, you can access the best hyperparameters and their corresponding performance:

python

 code

```python
print("Best hyperparameters: ", study.best_params)
print("Best accuracy: ", study.best_value)
```

5. Pruning Unpromising Trials

Optuna supports pruning to automatically stop unpromising trials based on intermediate results. To enable pruning, you need to define a pruning callback in your training loop.

Example with Pruning

python

 code

```python
def objective(trial):
    model = MyModel(...)
    for step in range(100):
```

```
model.train(...)
intermediate_value = model.evaluate(...)

# Report intermediate results
trial.report(intermediate_value, step)

# Check if the trial should be pruned
if trial.should_prune():
    raise optuna.exceptions.TrialPruned()
```

6. Visualizing Optimization Results

Optuna provides several visualization functions to analyze the optimization process. For example, you can visualize the optimization history and parameter importance:

python

code

```
import optuna.visualization as vis

# Plot the optimization history
vis.plot_optimization_history(study)

# Plot parameter importance
vis.plot_param_importances(study)
```

Real-World Applications of Optuna

1. Model Optimization

Optuna is widely used in both research and production settings to optimize hyperparameters for various machine learning models, including neural networks, decision trees, and more.

2. Automated Machine Learning (AutoML)

In AutoML frameworks, Optuna can be integrated to automatically search for optimal hyperparameters, reducing the need for manual tuning.

3. Ensemble Methods

Optuna is particularly useful for tuning ensemble methods, where multiple models are combined, and finding the best hyperparameters can significantly improve performance.

4. Deep Learning

Optuna can optimize hyperparameters in deep learning applications, including learning rates, batch sizes, and architecture-specific parameters.

Conclusion

Optuna is a powerful and flexible framework for hyperparameter optimization, offering advanced features such as automatic pruning and dynamic search spaces. Its ease of use and integration with popular machine learning libraries make it an invaluable tool for data scientists and machine learning practitioners.

By leveraging Optuna in your machine learning workflows, you can automate the tuning process, improve model performance, and ultimately save time and computational resources, leading to more effective and efficient ML solutions.

Ray Tune: A Comprehensive Overview of Scalable Hyperparameter Tuning

Introduction to Ray Tune

Ray Tune is a scalable hyperparameter tuning library built on top of Ray, a distributed computing framework. It provides a flexible and efficient way to optimize hyperparameters for machine learning models, allowing practitioners to leverage parallel and distributed computing to speed up the tuning process. Ray Tune integrates seamlessly with popular machine learning libraries, making it a versatile tool for hyperparameter optimization across various frameworks.

Key Features of Ray Tune

1. **Scalability**: Designed for distributed and parallel hyperparameter tuning, enabling large-scale experimentation.
2. **Integration**: Works with popular ML libraries like TensorFlow, PyTorch, and Scikit-learn.
3. **Flexible Search Algorithms**: Supports a wide range of optimization algorithms, including grid search, random search, Bayesian optimization, and more.
4. **Automatic Resource Management**: Efficiently allocates resources across trials to maximize utilization.
5. **Checkpointing and Resuming**: Supports trial checkpointing, allowing experiments to resume after interruptions.

Core Components of Ray Tune

1. Installation

You can install Ray Tune using pip:

bash

code

```
pip install ray[tune]
```

2. Basic Usage

To use Ray Tune, you need to define a training function that accepts hyperparameters and returns a metric to optimize. Here's a simple example:

Defining a Training Function

python

code

```
import ray
from ray import tune

def train_model(config):
    model = MyModel(n_estimators=config["n_estimators"], learning_rate=config["learning_rate"])
    model.fit(X_train, y_train)
    accuracy = model.evaluate(X_val, y_val)
```

```python
tune.report(accuracy=accuracy)
```

3. Running the Optimization

To perform hyperparameter tuning, you can use the tune.run method, specifying the training function and the search space for hyperparameters:

python

 code

```python
analysis = tune.run(
    train_model,
    config={
        "n_estimators": tune.randint(10, 100),
        "learning_rate": tune.uniform(0.001, 0.1),
    },
    num_samples=100,
    resources_per_trial={"cpu": 1, "gpu": 0.5}  # Customize resources
)
```

4. Accessing the Results

After the tuning process, you can access the best hyperparameters and their corresponding performance metrics:

python

 code

```python
print("Best hyperparameters: ", analysis.best_config)
print("Best accuracy: ", analysis.best_result["accuracy"])
```

5. Advanced Search Algorithms

Ray Tune supports various advanced search algorithms for hyperparameter tuning, including:

- **Bayesian Optimization**: Efficiently searches the hyperparameter space using past trial results.
- **Population-Based Training (PBT)**: Continuously adapts hyperparameters during training based on model performance.
- **ASHA (Asynchronous Successive Halving Algorithm)**: Automatically prunes unpromising trials based on intermediate results.

Example with Bayesian Optimization

```python
from ray.tune.suggest.bayesian import BayesianOptimization

bayes_search = BayesianOptimization(metric="accuracy", mode="max")
analysis = tune.run(
    train_model,
    search_alg=bayes_search,
    num_samples=50,
)
```

6. Integration with Popular Frameworks

Ray Tune integrates seamlessly with popular machine learning libraries, allowing you to leverage its capabilities without significant changes to your workflow. Here's a quick example of using Ray Tune with TensorFlow:

TensorFlow Example

```python
from ray import tune
from ray.tune.integration.keras import TuneReporter

def train_tf_model(config):
    model = build_model(config)
    model.fit(X_train, y_train, callbacks=[TuneReporter(metrics={"accuracy": "val_accuracy"})])

analysis = tune.run(
    train_tf_model,
    config={
        "learning_rate": tune.loguniform(1e-4, 1e-1),
        "batch_size": tune.choice([16, 32, 64]),
    },
```

)

Real-World Applications of Ray Tune

1. Large-Scale Hyperparameter Optimization

Ray Tune is particularly useful for projects requiring extensive hyperparameter tuning across multiple models, efficiently handling large search spaces and numerous trials.

2. Automated Machine Learning (AutoML)

In AutoML contexts, Ray Tune can be integrated to automate hyperparameter searches, significantly reducing the time needed for model optimization.

3. Distributed Training

Ray Tune's ability to scale across multiple nodes makes it ideal for hyperparameter tuning in environments where distributed training is essential, such as cloud-based setups.

4. Real-Time Experimentation

With its support for advanced search algorithms and adaptive methods, Ray Tune allows for real-time experimentation and optimization, providing immediate feedback on model performance.

Conclusion

Ray Tune is a powerful and scalable framework for hyperparameter tuning, offering a wide range of features that simplify the optimization process in machine learning. Its integration with popular libraries, support for advanced search algorithms, and ability to scale across distributed systems make it an invaluable tool for data scientists and machine learning practitioners.

By incorporating Ray Tune into your machine learning workflow, you can efficiently optimize hyperparameters, improve model performance, and save time on extensive manual tuning processes, ultimately leading to better and more efficient ML solutions.

OpenAI Gym:

A Comprehensive Overview of Reinforcement Learning Toolkit

Introduction to OpenAI Gym

OpenAI Gym is a popular toolkit designed for developing and comparing reinforcement learning (RL) algorithms. It provides a wide variety of environments where agents can be trained and evaluated, making it a crucial resource for researchers and practitioners in the field of machine learning. Gym's simplicity and extensibility enable users to easily implement, test, and benchmark different RL algorithms across diverse scenarios.

Key Features of OpenAI Gym

1. **Variety of Environments**: Offers a wide range of environments, from classic control tasks to Atari games and robotics simulations.

2. **Standardized API**: Provides a consistent interface for all environments, simplifying the process of switching between different tasks.

3. **Extensibility**: Allows users to create custom environments and integrate them seamlessly with existing Gym interfaces.

4. **Support for Multiple Frameworks**: Easily integrates with popular deep learning libraries like TensorFlow and PyTorch.

5. **Community and Resources**: Supported by a vibrant community and numerous tutorials, papers, and resources for learning and experimentation.

Core Components of OpenAI Gym

1. Installation

You can install OpenAI Gym using pip. Depending on the environments you wish to use, you may need to install additional packages:

bash

code

pip install gym

For environments like Atari, you can install the required dependencies:

bash

 code

pip install gym[atari]

2. Basic Usage

To get started with OpenAI Gym, you need to create an environment, reset it, and then interact with it by taking actions and receiving feedback.

Creating and Interacting with an Environment

Here's a simple example using the classic CartPole environment:

python

 code

```
import gym

# Create the environment
env = gym.make('CartPole-v1')

# Reset the environment to start
state = env.reset()

for _ in range(1000):
    env.render()  # Render the environment
    action = env.action_space.sample()  # Sample a random action
    state, reward, done, info = env.step(action)  # Take a step

    if done:
        break

env.close()  # Close the environment
```

3. Environment Structure

OpenAI Gym environments follow a consistent API:

- **env.reset()**: Resets the environment to an initial state and returns the first observation.
- **env.step(action)**: Takes an action in the environment and returns:
  - The next state
  - The reward received after taking the action
  - A boolean indicating whether the episode has ended
  - Additional information (optional)
- **env.render()**: Renders the environment for visualization (if applicable).
- **env.close()**: Closes the environment.

4. Creating Custom Environments

OpenAI Gym allows you to create your own environments by subclassing the gym.Env class. You need to implement four main methods: __init__(), reset(), step(), and render().

Example of a Custom Environment

python

code

```
import gym
from gym import spaces

class CustomEnv(gym.Env):
    def __init__(self):
        super(CustomEnv, self).__init__()
        self.action_space = spaces.Discrete(2)  # Example: two discrete actions
        self.observation_space = spaces.Box(low=0, high=1, shape=(3,), dtype=float)

    def reset(self):
        return self.observation_space.sample()  # Return a random state

    def step(self, action):
        # Implement your step logic
        next_state = self.observation_space.sample()
        reward = 1.0  # Example reward
        done = False  # Example termination condition
```

```
        return next_state, reward, done, {}

    def render(self, mode='human'):
        pass  # Implement rendering logic if needed
```

5. Integration with Reinforcement Learning Libraries

OpenAI Gym can be easily integrated with popular reinforcement learning libraries, such as Stable Baselines3, which provides implementations of various RL algorithms.

Example of Using Stable Baselines3 with Gym

python

code

```python
import gym
from stable_baselines3 import PPO

# Create the environment
env = gym.make('CartPole-v1')

# Create the model
model = PPO("MlpPolicy", env, verbose=1)

# Train the model
model.learn(total_timesteps=10000)

# Test the trained model
obs = env.reset()
for _ in range(1000):
    action, _states = model.predict(obs)
    obs, rewards, done, info = env.step(action)
    env.render()
    if done:
        break
```

env.close()

Real-World Applications of OpenAI Gym

1. Research in Reinforcement Learning

OpenAI Gym is widely used in academic and industrial research to develop and benchmark new RL algorithms, providing a common platform for comparison.

2. Educational Resources

The simplicity and flexibility of OpenAI Gym make it an excellent resource for teaching and learning reinforcement learning concepts, with many tutorials and examples available.

3. Game Development

Developers use OpenAI Gym to test and refine RL algorithms in gaming environments, allowing for the creation of intelligent agents in games.

4. Robotics and Control Systems

OpenAI Gym provides simulation environments for robotics tasks, enabling the development of algorithms for real-world applications in robotics and control systems.

Conclusion

OpenAI Gym is a vital toolkit for anyone interested in reinforcement learning. Its variety of environments, standardized API, and extensibility make it an essential resource for researchers, educators, and practitioners alike. By leveraging OpenAI Gym, you can effectively develop, test, and compare reinforcement learning algorithms, ultimately advancing your understanding and application of this exciting field.

Stable Baselines3: A Comprehensive Overview of Reinforcement Learning Implementations

Introduction to Stable Baselines3

Stable Baselines3 (SB3) is a popular library for reinforcement learning (RL) that provides implementations of state-of-the-art algorithms built on PyTorch. It aims to simplify the development and deployment of RL algorithms by offering a clean, user-friendly interface and well-documented code. SB3 is widely used in both research and production settings, making it an essential tool for anyone working in the field of reinforcement learning.

Key Features of Stable Baselines3

1. **Easy to Use**: A high-level interface that abstracts away many complexities of RL, allowing users to focus on model design and experimentation.

2. **Comprehensive Documentation**: Extensive documentation and examples make it easy for newcomers to get started and understand the algorithms.

3. **Multiple Algorithms**: Implements a variety of popular RL algorithms, including PPO, DDPG, A2C, TRPO, and SAC.

4. **Integration with OpenAI Gym**: Seamless integration with OpenAI Gym environments allows for easy experimentation and evaluation.

5. **Customizability**: Flexibility to modify and extend existing algorithms according to specific needs.

Core Components of Stable Baselines3

1. Installation

You can install Stable Baselines3 via pip:

bash

 code

pip install stable-baselines3[extra]

This command includes extra dependencies for working with various environments.

2. Basic Usage

To get started with Stable Baselines3, you typically follow these steps: create an environment, choose an RL algorithm, create a model, and train it.

Example with Proximal Policy Optimization (PPO)

Here's a simple example demonstrating how to use Stable Baselines3 with the PPO algorithm:

python

 code

import gym

from stable_baselines3 import PPO

```python
# Create the environment
env = gym.make('CartPole-v1')

# Create the PPO model
model = PPO("MlpPolicy", env, verbose=1)

# Train the model
model.learn(total_timesteps=10000)

# Save the model
model.save("ppo_cartpole")

# Load the model
model = PPO.load("ppo_cartpole")

# Test the trained model
obs = env.reset()
for _ in range(1000):
    action, _states = model.predict(obs)
    obs, rewards, done, info = env.step(action)
    env.render()
    if done:
        obs = env.reset()

env.close()
```

3. Supported Algorithms

Stable Baselines3 implements several reinforcement learning algorithms, including:

- **PPO (Proximal Policy Optimization)**: A widely used on-policy algorithm that is stable and efficient.
- **A2C (Advantage Actor-Critic)**: An on-policy algorithm that uses both policy and value function approximations.

- **DDPG (Deep Deter-stic Policy Gradient)**: An off-policy algorithm suitable for continuous action spaces.
- **SAC (Soft Actor-Critic)**: An off-policy algorithm that combines the benefits of actor-critic and entropy regularization.
- **TRPO (Trust Region Policy Optimization)**: An advanced on-policy algorithm designed to ensure small updates to the policy.

4. Customizing Models

Stable Baselines3 allows users to customize various components of the models, including the neural network architecture, learning rate, and more.

Example of Customizing Policy Network

You can define a custom neural network for your policy as follows:

python

code

```python
from stable_baselines3.common.policies import MlpPolicy

class CustomMlpPolicy(MlpPolicy):
    def __init__(self, *args, **kwargs):
        super(CustomMlpPolicy, self).__init__(*args, **kwargs)

# Train the model with a custom policy
model = PPO(CustomMlpPolicy, env, verbose=1)
model.learn(total_timesteps=10000)
```

5. Evaluation and Callback Functions

Stable Baselines3 provides tools for evaluating model performance and using callback functions to monitor training.

Evaluating the Model

You can evaluate the performance of your trained model using the evaluate function:

python

code

```python
from stable_baselines3.common.evaluation import evaluate_policy

mean_reward, std_reward = evaluate_policy(model, env, n_eval_episodes=10)
```

print(f"Mean reward: {mean_reward} +/- {std_reward}")

Using Callbacks

You can also define custom callbacks to save models or log training metrics during training:

python

 code

```
from stable_baselines3.common.callbacks import BaseCallback

class CustomCallback(BaseCallback):
    def __init__(self, verbose=0):
        super(CustomCallback, self).__init__(verbose)

    def _on_step(self) -> bool:
        # Custom logic for each step
        return True

# Train with the custom callback
model.learn(total_timesteps=10000, callback=CustomCallback())
```

Real-World Applications of Stable Baselines3

1. Research and Development

SB3 is widely used in academic research to experiment with and benchmark new reinforcement learning algorithms and techniques.

2. Industrial Applications

Companies leverage Stable Baselines3 for real-world applications in robotics, autonomous vehicles, game AI, and more, benefiting from the library's ease of use and robustness.

3. Educational Resources

Stable Baselines3 serves as an excellent resource for teaching reinforcement learning concepts, offering clear examples and a user-friendly API for students and educators.

4. Game Development

Developers utilize SB3 to create intelligent agents that can learn to play games, either for research or for enhancing game experiences.

Conclusion

Stable Baselines3 is a powerful and user-friendly library for reinforcement learning that simplifies the implementation of state-of-the-art algorithms. Its extensive documentation, support for multiple algorithms, and seamless integration with OpenAI Gym make it an invaluable resource for researchers, educators, and practitioners in the field.

By using Stable Baselines3, you can effectively experiment with and deploy reinforcement learning models, leading to more efficient and effective solutions across a wide range of applications. Whether you are a beginner or an experienced researcher, SB3 provides the tools you need to advance your work in reinforcement learning.

Jupyter Notebooks: A Comprehensive Overview of

Interactive Research and Collaboration Tools

Introduction to Jupyter Notebooks

Jupyter Notebooks are a powerful tool for interactive computing that facilitate research, documentation, and collaboration in data science and scientific computing. They provide an intuitive web-based interface where users can create and share documents that contain live code, equations, visualizations, and narrative text. Jupyter Notebooks have become an essential resource in academia and industry, enabling researchers and practitioners to document their work, experiment with code, and communicate findings effectively.

Key Features of Jupyter Notebooks

1. **Interactive Code Execution**: Run code in real-time, allowing for immediate feedback and experimentation.

2. **Rich Text Support**: Combine code with Markdown, enabling the inclusion of formatted text, images, links, and LaTeX for mathematical expressions.

3. **Visualization Capabilities**: Easily integrate visualizations from libraries like Matplotlib, Seaborn, and Plotly directly within the notebook.

4. **Kernel Support**: Support for multiple programming languages through different kernels, including Python, R, Julia, and more.

5. **Export Options**: Export notebooks in various formats, such as HTML, PDF, and Markdown, for easy sharing and publication.

Core Components of Jupyter Notebooks

1. Installation

You can install Jupyter Notebooks via Anaconda or pip. Here's how to install it using pip:

bash

 code

pip install notebook

To start the Jupyter Notebook server, run:

bash

code

jupyter notebook

This command will open a new tab in your web browser where you can create and manage notebooks.

2. Notebook Interface

The Jupyter Notebook interface consists of several key components:

- **Cells**: The building blocks of a notebook. Cells can contain code, Markdown text, or raw text.
- **Toolbar**: Provides buttons for common actions, such as saving, adding cells, and running code.
- **Kernel**: The computational engine that executes the code contained in the notebook. You can choose from different kernels based on the programming language.

3. Working with Cells

Code Cells

Code cells allow you to write and execute code. You can run a code cell by selecting it and clicking the "Run" button or pressing Shift + Enter.

python

code

Example code cell

import numpy as np

Create an array

array = np.array([1, 2, 3, 4])

print(array)

Markdown Cells

Markdown cells enable you to write formatted text, including headings, lists, links, and images. You can include LaTeX for mathematical notation as well.

markdown

code

This is a Heading

Here's a list of items:

- Item 1

- Item 2

Here's a mathematical equation: $(E = mc^2)$

4. Visualizations

Jupyter Notebooks integrate seamlessly with popular visualization libraries. For example, you can create and display plots using Matplotlib:

python

 code

```
import matplotlib.pyplot as plt

# Simple plot
plt.plot(array)
plt.title("Example Plot")
plt.xlabel("Index")
plt.ylabel("Value")
plt.show()
```

5. Extensions and Customization

Jupyter Notebooks support various extensions that enhance functionality, such as:

- **JupyterLab**: An advanced interface with improved file management and layout options.
- **nbextensions**: A collection of community-contributed extensions that add features like table of contents, code folding, and more.

You can install JupyterLab with:

bash

 code

```
pip install jupyterlab
```

6. Collaboration and Sharing

Jupyter Notebooks can be easily shared with others. You can export notebooks in different formats (e.g., HTML, PDF) or share them directly using platforms like GitHub or Jupyter Notebook Viewer.

For collaborative work, tools like **JupyterHub** and **Google Colab** allow multiple users to work on notebooks simultaneously.

Real-World Applications of Jupyter Notebooks

1. Data Analysis and Visualization

Jupyter Notebooks are widely used for exploratory data analysis, allowing data scientists to visualize datasets interactively and document their findings.

2. Machine Learning and Model Development

Researchers use Jupyter Notebooks to develop, train, and evaluate machine learning models, providing a comprehensive view of the process from data preprocessing to model evaluation.

3. Educational Resources

Jupyter Notebooks serve as excellent teaching tools for programming, data science, and machine learning, allowing students to engage with interactive content and learn through experimentation.

4. Scientific Research

Academics leverage Jupyter Notebooks to document and share research findings, enabling reproducibility and collaboration within the scientific community.

Conclusion

Jupyter Notebooks have transformed the way researchers, data scientists, and educators work with code and data. Their interactive nature, rich text support, and powerful visualization capabilities make them an essential tool for documenting research, conducting experiments, and sharing findings.

By utilizing Jupyter Notebooks, you can enhance your productivity, foster collaboration, and create engaging educational materials, ultimately advancing your work in data science and scientific computing. Whether you are a beginner or an experienced practitioner, Jupyter Notebooks provide the flexibility and functionality you need to succeed in your projects.

Git: A Comprehensive Overview of Version Control and Collaboration

Introduction to Git

Git is a distributed version control system designed to track changes in source code during software development. It allows multiple developers to collaborate on projects efficiently, managing changes, branches, and version history seamlessly. Git's robustness, speed, and flexibility make it the de facto standard for version control in both open-source and commercial projects.

Key Features of Git

1. **Distributed Architecture**: Every developer has a full copy of the repository, enabling offline work and easy collaboration.

2. **Branching and Merging**: Supports multiple branches for feature development, allowing parallel work without affecting the main codebase.

3. **Staging Area**: Provides a staging area to prepare commits, giving developers control over what changes are included in each commit.

4. **History Tracking**: Maintains a detailed history of changes, making it easy to review past versions, identify authors, and revert to previous states.

5. **Collaboration**: Facilitates collaboration through pull requests, code reviews, and integration with platforms like GitHub and GitLab.

Core Components of Git

1. Installation

You can install Git on various operating systems. Here's how to install it on common platforms:

- **Windows**: Download and run the installer from the official Git website.
- **macOS**: Install via Homebrew:

bash

 code

brew install git

- **Linux**: Install using package managers (e.g., apt, yum):

bash

 code

sudo apt-get install git

2. Basic Commands

Here are some fundamental Git commands for managing repositories:

Creating a Repository

To create a new Git repository, navigate to your project directory and run:

bash

 code

git init

Cloning a Repository

To clone an existing repository:

bash

 code

git clone <repository-url>

Checking Status

To check the status of your repository:

bash

 code

git status

Adding Changes

To stage changes for commit:

bash

```
code
git add <file-or-directory>
```

Committing Changes

To commit staged changes with a message:

bash

```code
git commit -m "Your commit message"
```

Pushing Changes

To push your commits to a remote repository:

bash

```code
git push origin <branch-name>
```

Pulling Changes

To fetch and merge changes from a remote repository:

bash

```code
git pull origin <branch-name>
```

3. Branching and Merging

Git allows you to create branches for different features or experiments. Here's how to manage branches:

Creating a Branch

To create a new branch:

bash

```code
git branch <branch-name>
```

Switching Branches

To switch to a different branch:

bash

```code
git checkout <branch-name>
```

Merging Branches

To merge changes from one branch into another:

bash

 code

git checkout <target-branch>

git merge <source-branch>

4. Collaboration Workflow

A common workflow when collaborating on a project includes:

1. **Forking**: Fork the original repository to create your own copy.
2. **Cloning**: Clone your forked repository to your local machine.
3. **Creating a Feature Branch**: Create a new branch for your changes.
4. **Making Changes**: Make your changes, commit, and push them to your fork.
5. **Creating a Pull Request**: Submit a pull request to the original repository for review.

Real-World Applications of Git

1. Software Development

Git is the backbone of modern software development, enabling teams to collaborate on code efficiently and manage project histories.

2. Open-Source Projects

Many open-source projects use Git for version control, allowing contributors to collaborate globally, submit patches, and maintain code quality through reviews.

3. Continuous Integration/Continuous Deployment (CI/CD)

Git is often integrated with CI/CD pipelines, enabling automated testing and deployment processes based on version changes.

4. Documentation and Content Management

Git can also be used for version control of documentation, ensuring that changes are tracked and previous versions can be accessed easily.

Conclusion

Git is an essential tool for version control and collaboration, empowering developers to manage code changes, collaborate efficiently, and maintain a clear history of their projects. By mastering Git, you can enhance your productivity, streamline your workflows, and contribute effectively to team projects, whether in open-source or commercial environments.

Google Colab: A Comprehensive Overview of Cloud-Based Jupyter Notebook Service

Introduction to Google Colab

Google Colab, or "Colaboratory," is a cloud-based Jupyter notebook service provided by Google that allows users to write, execute, and share code in an interactive environment. Colab is especially popular in data science, machine learning, and deep learning due to its ease of use, collaboration features, and free access to powerful computing resources, including GPUs.

Key Features of Google Colab

1. **Free GPU and TPU Access**: Provides free access to powerful GPUs and TPUs, enabling faster computation for machine learning tasks.

2. **Easy Sharing and Collaboration**: Users can share notebooks easily via Google Drive, allowing for real-time collaboration and feedback.

3. **Integration with Google Services**: Seamlessly integrates with Google Drive, Google Sheets, and other Google services for data storage and retrieval.

4. **Rich Ecosystem**: Supports popular libraries like TensorFlow, PyTorch, and NumPy, making it suitable for a variety of applications.

5. **No Setup Required**: Eliminates the need for local installation, allowing users to start coding immediately in a web browser.

Core Components of Google Colab

1. Getting Started

To use Google Colab, simply go to the Colab website and sign in with your Google account. You can create a new notebook or open an existing one from Google Drive or GitHub.

2. Notebook Interface

The Google Colab interface is similar to Jupyter Notebooks and includes:

- **Code Cells**: Where you write and execute code.
- **Text Cells**: Where you can write formatted text using Markdown.
- **Toolbar**: Provides options for running cells, inserting code or text cells, and sharing the notebook.

3. Running Code

You can execute code cells by clicking the play button or pressing Shift + Enter. Colab supports various libraries and frameworks, allowing you to perform data analysis, machine learning, and more.

Example: Running Simple Code

python

 code

import numpy as np

```
# Create an array
array = np.array([1, 2, 3, 4])
print(array)
```

4. Using GPUs and TPUs

To leverage GPU or TPU acceleration in Google Colab, go to Runtime > Change runtime type and select either GPU or TPU as the hardware accelerator. This significantly speeds up computations for tasks like training deep learning models.

5. Importing Data

You can import data from various sources, such as Google Drive, GitHub, or directly from the web. For instance, to mount Google Drive:

python

 code

```
from google.colab import drive
drive.mount('/content/drive')
```

6. Sharing and Collaboration

Google Colab makes it easy to share notebooks. You can share a link directly or invite collaborators via email. Collaboration features allow multiple users to edit the notebook simultaneously.

Real-World Applications of Google Colab

1. Data Science and Machine Learning

Colab is widely used for data analysis, model training, and experimentation in data science and machine learning due to its easy setup and powerful computational resources.

2. Education and Tutorials

Many educators use Google Colab for teaching programming, data science, and machine learning, as it allows students to engage with interactive content without setup hassles.

3. Prototyping and Experimentation

Researchers and developers leverage Colab to quickly prototype ideas and run experiments, especially when they require significant computational power.

4. Sharing Results

Colab notebooks are often used to share research results and analyses, allowing others to reproduce findings and collaborate effectively.

Conclusion

Google Colab is a versatile and powerful tool for anyone involved in data science, machine learning, or programming. With its free access to GPUs, easy sharing capabilities, and integration with Google services, Colab provides an ideal environment for experimentation, collaboration, and learning. Whether you are a student, researcher, or developer, Google Colab can significantly enhance your workflow and productivity.

AIF360 (AI Fairness 360): A Comprehensive Overview of Tools for Ethical AI

Introduction to AIF360

AI Fairness 360 (AIF360) is an open-source library developed by IBM that provides a comprehensive suite of tools for detecting and mitigating bias in machine learning models. As machine learning systems increasingly influence important decisions in various sectors—such as hiring, lending, and law enforcement—ensuring fairness and ethical considerations in these models has become crucial. AIF360 offers algorithms and metrics designed to help practitioners assess and improve the fairness of their models, making it an essential resource in the field of responsible AI.

Key Features of AIF360

1. **Bias Detection**: Provides various metrics to assess bias in datasets and model predictions, enabling practitioners to identify potential sources of unfairness.

2. **Mitigation Algorithms**: Includes algorithms for mitigating bias at different stages of the machine learning pipeline—pre-processing, in-processing, and post-processing.

3. **Comprehensive Documentation**: Offers detailed documentation and tutorials, making it accessible for both newcomers and experienced practitioners.

4. **Interoperability**: Works with popular machine learning libraries, such as TensorFlow and Scikit-learn, allowing for seamless integration into existing workflows.

5. **Community Support**: As an open-source project, AIF360 benefits from contributions and feedback from the broader AI ethics community.

Core Components of AIF360

1. Installation

AIF360 can be easily installed via pip:

bash

 code

pip install aif360

2. Bias Detection Metrics

AIF360 provides a range of metrics for detecting bias in datasets and model predictions. Some common metrics include:

- **Statistical Parity Difference**: Measures the difference in positive prediction rates between different demographic groups.
- **Equal Opportunity Difference**: Assesses the difference in true positive rates between groups.
- **Disparate Impact**: Evaluates the ratio of favorable outcomes for different demographic groups.

Example: Calculating Bias Metrics

Here's how to calculate bias metrics using AIF360:

python

 code

```
from aif360.datasets import BinaryLabelDataset
from aif360.metrics import BinaryLabelDatasetMetric

# Load your dataset
dataset = BinaryLabelDataset(...)

# Calculate metrics
metric = BinaryLabelDatasetMetric(dataset, privileged_groups=[...], unprivileged_groups=[...])
print("Statistical Parity Difference:", metric.statistical_parity_difference())
```

3. Mitigation Algorithms

AIF360 offers several mitigation algorithms that can be applied at different stages of the machine learning workflow:

Pre-processing Techniques

These methods modify the training dataset to remove bias before model training. Examples include:

- **Reweighing**: Adjusts the weights of instances in the dataset to balance the representation of different groups.
- **Disentangled Representation Learning**: Learns representations that separate sensitive attributes from other features.

In-processing Techniques

These methods modify the learning algorithm itself during training. Examples include:

- **Adversarial Debiasing**: Uses adversarial training to -mize bias while maximizing predictive accuracy.
- **Fair Logistic Regression**: Incorporates fairness constraints into the logistic regression model.

Post-processing Techniques

These methods adjust model predictions after training. Examples include:

- **Equalized Odds Post-processing**: Adjusts the predictions to ensure equalized odds across groups.
- **Calibrated Equalized Odds**: Ensures that the predicted probabilities are calibrated while satisfying fairness constraints.

Example: Using a Mitigation Algorithm

Here's how to use a reweighing technique to mitigate bias:

python

code

```
from aif360.algorithms.preprocessing import Reweighing

# Apply reweighing
rw = Reweighing(unprivileged_groups=[...], privileged_groups=[...])
dataset_transformed = rw.fit_transform(dataset)
```

4. Integration with Machine Learning Workflows

AIF360 is designed to integrate seamlessly with popular machine learning frameworks. You can use it alongside TensorFlow, PyTorch, and Scikit-learn to ensure fairness throughout your model training and evaluation process.

5. Case Studies and Applications

AIF360 provides example notebooks that demonstrate how to apply bias detection and mitigation techniques to real-world datasets. These case studies can serve as valuable resources for understanding how to implement ethical AI practices in various domains.

Real-World Applications of AIF360

1. Hiring Processes

Organizations can use AIF360 to evaluate and mitigate bias in their recruitment algorithms, ensuring fair treatment of candidates from diverse backgrounds.

2. Loan Approvals

Financial institutions can employ AIF360 to assess bias in their credit scoring models, helping to prevent discriminatory lending practices.

3. Criminal Justice

Law enforcement agencies can utilize AIF360 to examine risk assessment tools, ensuring that they do not disproportionately affect specific demographic groups.

4. Healthcare

Healthcare systems can apply AIF360 to ensure that predictive models for patient outcomes do not exhibit bias, ultimately leading to fairer treatment options.

Conclusion

AI Fairness 360 is a powerful toolkit for researchers and practitioners committed to ethical AI practices. By providing robust methods for detecting and mitigating bias, AIF360 empowers users to build more fair and responsible machine learning systems. As the demand for transparency and accountability in AI continues to grow, tools like AIF360 will play a crucial role in ensuring that AI technologies are developed and deployed responsibly, promoting equity and fairness in various domains.

Fairlearn: A Comprehensive Overview of a Toolkit for Fairness in Machine Learning

Introduction to Fairlearn

Fairlearn is an open-source toolkit designed to assist machine learning practitioners in assessing and mitigating unfairness in their models. As the impact of machine learning systems grows across various sectors—such as finance, healthcare, and law enforcement—the need for fairness and equity in these systems has become increasingly important. Fairlearn provides algorithms and tools that help evaluate model performance across different demographic groups, enabling developers to create fairer AI systems.

Key Features of Fairlearn

1. **Bias Assessment**: Fairlearn offers metrics to evaluate the fairness of machine learning models, allowing practitioners to identify and quantify biases in their predictions.

2. **Mitigation Techniques**: The toolkit includes algorithms for mitigating bias both during model training (in-processing) and after predictions are made (post-processing).

3. **User-Friendly API**: Designed to be intuitive and easy to integrate with popular machine learning frameworks such as Scikit-learn, making it accessible for a wide range of users.

4. **Interactive Visualization**: Provides visual tools to help understand the fairness of models and the effects of mitigation strategies.

5. **Comprehensive Documentation**: Detailed documentation and examples are available, making it easier for users to implement fairness measures in their projects.

Core Components of Fairlearn

1. Installation

You can easily install Fairlearn using pip:

bash

 code

pip install fairlearn

2. Bias Assessment Metrics

Fairlearn provides several metrics to evaluate model fairness across different groups. Some of the key metrics include:

- **Demographic Parity**: Measures whether the prediction rates are equal across different demographic groups.
- **Equal Opportunity**: Assesses whether true positive rates are equal across groups.
- **Calibration**: Evaluates whether predicted probabilities correspond accurately to actual outcomes across groups.

Example: Calculating Fairness Metrics

Here's how to calculate fairness metrics using Fairlearn:

python

 code

```
from fairlearn.metrics import (
    MetricFrame,
    demographic_parity_difference,
)


# Assume y_true and y_pred are your true labels and predictions
metric_frame = MetricFrame(metrics=demographic_parity_difference,
                y_true=y_true,
                y_pred=y_pred,
                sensitive_features=sensitive_features)
```

print(metric_frame.overall)

3. Mitigation Techniques

Fairlearn includes several algorithms for mitigating bias. These can be broadly categorized into two types: in-processing and post-processing techniques.

In-Processing Techniques

These methods adjust the training process to promote fairness:

- **Fairness-Constrained Classifiers**: Algorithms like the ExponentialClassifier that incorporate fairness constraints directly into the optimization process.

Post-Processing Techniques

These methods adjust model predictions after training:

- **Equalized Odds Post-processing**: This technique modifies the model's output to ensure that true positive rates are equal across different groups.

Example: Applying Mitigation Techniques

Here's how to use the ExponentialClassifier for in-processing mitigation:

python

code

```
from fairlearn.reductions import ExponentiatedGradient, DemographicParity

# Assume classifier is your base classifier and sensitive_features are defined
mitigator = ExponentiatedGradient(classifier, DemographicParity())
mitigator.fit(X_train, y_train, sensitive_features=sensitive_features)
y_pred_mitigated = mitigator.predict(X_test)
```

4. Interactive Visualization Tools

Fairlearn includes tools for visualizing the impact of different fairness metrics and mitigation strategies. This helps practitioners understand how changes affect model performance and fairness.

5. Case Studies and Examples

Fairlearn offers several example notebooks that demonstrate how to assess and mitigate bias using real-world datasets. These examples serve as a valuable resource for understanding practical applications of the toolkit.

Real-World Applications of Fairlearn

1. Hiring Algorithms

Organizations can use Fairlearn to assess bias in hiring algorithms, ensuring that candidates from diverse backgrounds are treated fairly and without discrimination.

2. Credit Scoring

Financial institutions can implement Fairlearn to evaluate their credit scoring models, helping to prevent biased lending practices that may disproportionately affect certain demographic groups.

3. Healthcare Decision-Making

Healthcare providers can apply Fairlearn to ensure that predictive models for patient outcomes are equitable, promoting fair treatment options across different populations.

4. Law Enforcement

Law enforcement agencies can use Fairlearn to analyze risk assessment tools, ensuring that they do not unfairly target specific communities.

Conclusion

Fairlearn is a powerful toolkit for promoting fairness and mitigating bias in machine learning systems. By providing accessible metrics and mitigation strategies, Fairlearn empowers practitioners to create more equitable AI solutions. As the demand for responsible AI continues to rise, tools like Fairlearn will play a critical role in ensuring that machine learning technologies benefit all communities fairly and justly. Through its comprehensive features and user-friendly design, Fairlearn serves as an essential resource for anyone committed to ethical AI practices.

DVC (Data Version Control): A

Comprehensive Overview of Data and Model Versioning

Introduction to DVC

Data Version Control (DVC) is an open-source version control system specifically designed for managing machine learning projects. As machine learning models become more complex and data-centric, the need for effective versioning of datasets, models, and experiments has grown. DVC provides tools to streamline the data management process, enabling teams to track changes, share datasets, and maintain reproducibility in their workflows.

Key Features of DVC

1. **Data and Model Versioning**: DVC allows users to version datasets and models similarly to how Git versions code, facilitating easy collaboration and tracking of changes.

2. **Reproducibility**: By tracking dependencies and experiments, DVC helps ensure that models can be reproduced reliably across different environments and setups.

3. **Large File Support**: DVC can handle large datasets that might not fit into a traditional Git repository, making it suitable for data-intensive projects.

4. **Integration with Git**: DVC works alongside Git, allowing users to manage code and data in a unified manner.

5. **Remote Storage Support**: DVC can connect to various cloud storage solutions (e.g., AWS S3, Google Drive, Azure Blob) to store data, making it easier to collaborate across teams.

Core Components of DVC

1. Installation

DVC can be easily installed using pip:

bash

 code

pip install dvc

2. Setting Up a DVC Project

To start a new DVC project, you need to initialize a Git repository and then initialize DVC within that repository:

bash

 code

git init

dvc init

This will create a .dvc directory where DVC configuration files are stored.

3. Tracking Data

To track a dataset with DVC, use the dvc add command. This command will create a .dvc file that contains metadata about the tracked data file:

bash

 code

dvc add data/my_dataset.csv

4. Data Remote Storage

DVC supports various remote storage backends for data storage. You can set up a remote storage location using:

bash

 code

dvc remote add -d myremote s3://mybucket/path

After setting up a remote, you can push your data to it:

bash

 code

dvc push

5. Versioning Models

Similar to datasets, you can track and version models. After training a model, you can register it with DVC:

bash

 code

dvc add models/my_model.pkl

6. Managing Experiments

DVC allows you to manage experiments effectively. You can create and run different versions of your ML pipeline with the dvc run command. This command helps define a reproducible pipeline with dependencies and outputs.

bash

code

```
dvc run -n my_experiment \
   -d data/my_dataset.csv \
   -o models/my_model.pkl \
   python train.py
```

7. Pipelines

DVC enables you to create pipelines to manage the entire machine learning workflow, from data preprocessing to model training and evaluation. You can define stages in your pipeline, and DVC will track the dependencies automatically.

8. Visualizing the Pipeline

DVC provides tools to visualize the pipeline, making it easier to understand the workflow and the relationships between different stages.

bash

code

```
dvc pipeline show --ascii
```

Real-World Applications of DVC

1. Collaborative Machine Learning

In teams where multiple data scientists and engineers work on different aspects of a project, DVC facilitates collaboration by providing version control for data and models, ensuring that everyone is on the same page.

2. Research and Development

Researchers can use DVC to manage experiments, keeping track of different versions of datasets and models, which is essential for reproducibility in scientific research.

3. Data Engineering

Data engineers can leverage DVC to manage data pipelines and ensure that data transformations are versioned, allowing for easier rollbacks and changes.

4. Continuous Integration/Continuous Deployment (CI/CD)

DVC can be integrated into CI/CD pipelines, ensuring that the latest versions of data and models are always tested and deployed in production environments.

Conclusion

DVC is an invaluable tool for managing datasets and machine learning models in a structured and reproducible manner. By providing capabilities for versioning, tracking, and collaboration, DVC empowers data scientists and machine learning engineers to focus on building better models while maintaining the integrity and reproducibility of their work. As the complexity of machine learning projects continues to grow, tools like DVC will play a critical role in streamlining workflows and ensuring successful outcomes.

Streamlit: A Comprehensive Overview for Creating Web Apps for ML Projects

Introduction to Streamlit

Streamlit is an open-source framework that allows developers to create interactive web applications for machine learning projects quickly and easily. Designed specifically for data scientists and machine learning practitioners, Streamlit streamlines the process of transforming data scripts into shareable web apps, making it simple to showcase results, visualize data, and interact with models without requiring extensive web development skills.

Key Features of Streamlit

1. **Simplicity and Ease of Use**: Streamlit's API is intuitive and allows for rapid development, enabling users to create apps with just a few lines of code.
2. **Real-time Interactivity**: Streamlit apps automatically update in real-time, providing an interactive experience for users as they adjust inputs or view outputs.
3. **Built-in Widgets**: The framework includes a variety of built-in widgets (like sliders, buttons, and text inputs) that enhance user interaction and engagement.
4. **Data Visualization**: Streamlit integrates seamlessly with popular data visualization libraries such as Matplotlib, Plotly, and Altair, allowing for dynamic visual representations of data.
5. **Easy Deployment**: Apps built with Streamlit can be easily deployed on various platforms, including Streamlit Sharing, Heroku, and AWS.

Core Components of Streamlit

1. Installation

Streamlit can be easily installed using pip:

bash

code

```
pip install streamlit
```

2. Basic App Structure

A simple Streamlit app consists of just a few lines of code. Here's a basic structure:

python

code

```
import streamlit as st

st.title("My First Streamlit App")
st.write("Hello, World!")
```

To run the app, save the script as app.py and execute:

bash

code

```
streamlit run app.py
```

3. Adding Widgets

Streamlit provides various widgets to make your app interactive. Here are some common widgets:

- **Text Input**: For user text input.

python

 code

```python
user_input = st.text_input("Enter some text:")
```

- **Slider**: For selecting numerical values.

python

 code

```python
slider_value = st.slider("Select a number", 0, 100)
```

- **Button**: To trigger actions.

python

 code

```python
if st.button("Submit"):
    st.write("You clicked the button!")
```

4. Data Visualization

Streamlit makes it easy to visualize data using various libraries. For instance, using Matplotlib:

python

 code

```python
import matplotlib.pyplot as plt

data = [1, 2, 3, 4]
plt.bar(range(len(data)), data)
st.pyplot(plt)
```

You can also use Plotly for interactive charts:

python

 code

```python
import plotly.express as px

fig = px.line(x=[1, 2, 3], y=[1, 3, 2], title="Sample Plot")
```

st.plotly_chart(fig)

5. Uploading and Processing Data

You can allow users to upload files directly through the app:

python

 code

```
uploaded_file = st.file_uploader("Choose a CSV file", type="csv")
if uploaded_file is not None:
    data = pd.read_csv(uploaded_file)
    st.write(data)
```

6. Caching for Performance

Streamlit includes a caching mechanism to improve performance, especially for data loading and processing functions. Use the @st.cache decorator:

python

 code

```
@st.cache
def load_data():
    # Simulate a data loading function
    return pd.read_csv('data.csv')

data = load_data()
```

7. Layouts and Customization

You can customize the layout of your app using columns and containers:

python

 code

```
col1, col2 = st.columns(2)
col1.header("Column 1")
col2.header("Column 2")
```

8. Deployment Options

Streamlit apps can be deployed easily on:

- **Streamlit Sharing**: A platform provided by Streamlit for hosting apps for free.

- **Heroku**: You can deploy your app on Heroku by following specific deployment steps.
- **Docker**: Create a Docker container for more controlled environments.

Real-World Applications of Streamlit

1. Data Exploration and Visualization

Data scientists can use Streamlit to create interactive dashboards that allow stakeholders to explore datasets dynamically, facilitating better data-driven decisions.

2. Model Deployment and Testing

Streamlit makes it easy to deploy machine learning models and create user-friendly interfaces for testing model predictions in real time.

3. Educational Tools

Educators can build interactive applications to demonstrate algorithms, data analysis techniques, or statistical concepts in an engaging manner.

4. Prototyping

Rapidly prototype machine learning applications and gather user feedback without extensive development overhead.

Conclusion

Streamlit is a powerful and accessible tool for creating interactive web applications tailored for machine learning projects. Its simplicity, real-time interactivity, and seamless integration with Python libraries make it an ideal choice for data scientists looking to showcase their work effectively. As the demand for user-friendly interfaces in machine learning continues to grow, Streamlit serves as a valuable resource for developers seeking to enhance collaboration and engagement in their projects.

www.ingramcontent.com/pod-product-compliance
Lightning Source LLC
Chambersburg PA
CBHW062104220526
45471CB00010B/3593